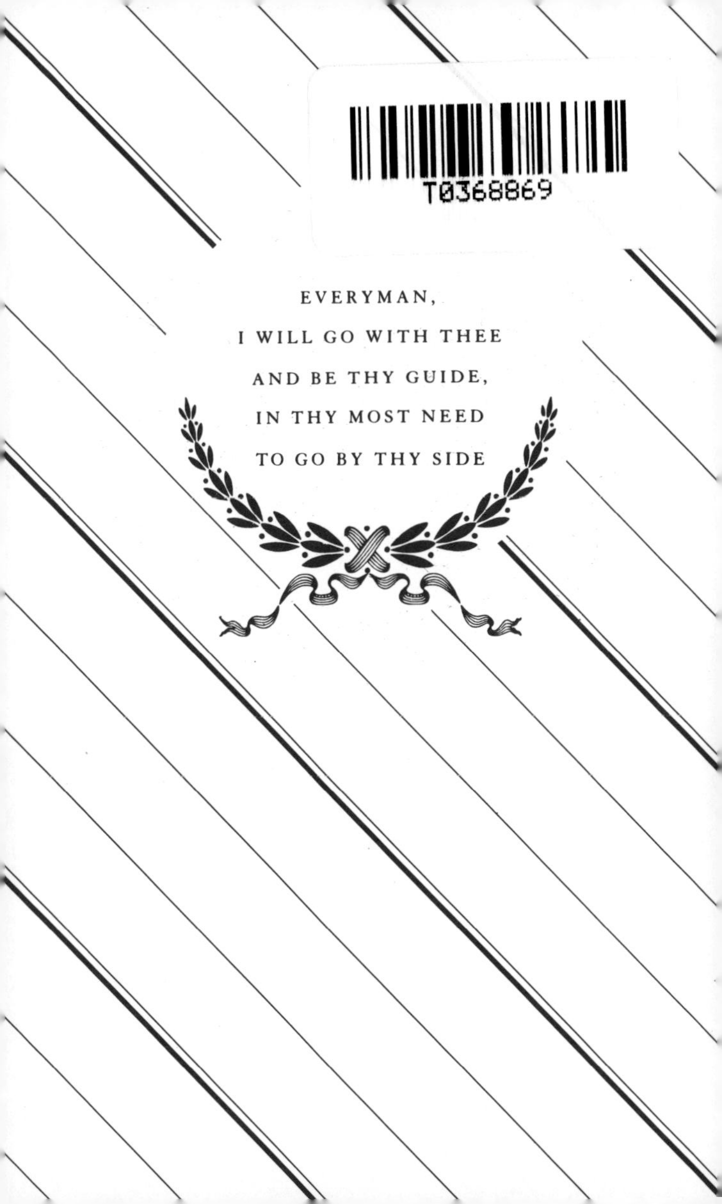
T0368869
EVERYMAN,
I WILL GO WITH THEE
AND BE THY GUIDE,
IN THY MOST NEED
TO GO BY THY SIDE

EVERYMAN'S LIBRARY

POCKET POETS

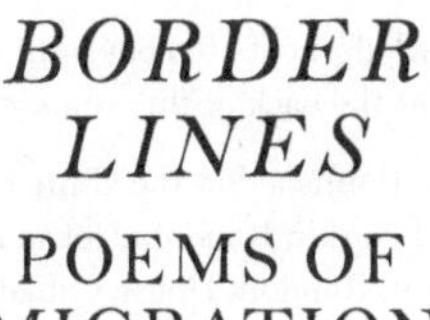

BORDER LINES

POEMS OF MIGRATION

EDITED BY

MIHAELA MOSCALIUC

AND MICHAEL WATERS

EVERYMAN'S LIBRARY

POCKET POETS

Alfred A. Knopf New York London Toronto

THIS IS A BORZOI BOOK

PUBLISHED BY ALFRED A. KNOPF

This selection by Mihaela Moscaliuc and Michael Waters first published in Everyman's Library, 2020

A list of acknowledgments to copyright owners appears at the back of this volume.

 Published in the United States by Alfred A. Knopf, a division of Penguin Random House LLC, New York, and in Canada by Penguin Random House Canada Limited, Toronto. Distributed by Penguin Random House LLC, New York. Published in the United Kingdom by Everyman's Library, 50 Albemarle Street, London W1S 4BD and distributed by Penguin Random House UK, 20 Vauxhall Bridge Road, London SW1V 2SA.

www.randomhouse/everymans
www.everymanslibrary.co.uk

ISBN 978-1-101-90824-2 (US)
978-1-84159-819-2 (UK)

A CIP catalogue record for this book is available from the British Library

Typography by Peter B. Willberg

Typeset in the UK by Input Data Services Ltd, Isle Abbotts, Somerset

Printed and bound in Germany by GGP Media GmbH, Possneck

CONTENTS

MOTHERLAND

LABOR

COMMUNITY

FOREWORD

The movement of peoples from one space to another, sometimes forcibly, as with the Middle Passage and the Trail of Tears, or courageously and voluntarily, as with the great migrations from Eastern Europe, Asia, and, more recently, Africa and Latin America to the United States and Western Europe, has been accompanied by immeasurable emotional and psychological displacements. Where is home? Is it the motherland, the left-behind world of birthplace and ancestry, or is it the strange but fresh landscape of possibility and promise? Which language articulates the private self, which the public? More recently, driven by war, poverty, and multiple forms of oppression, contexts shaped significantly by First World politics and interests, African and Middle Eastern peoples have risked their lives to touch the European continent, while Central Americans have journeyed north, all intent on crossing borders – pocked and cratered terrains, guarded rivers, dangerous and indifferent seas and oceans – toward more secure lives for themselves and their children. What is the cost of such unwilling or hopeful migration? "By the rivers of Babylon we sat and wept when we remembered Zion," writes the anonymous poet of Psalm 137.

Throughout the long history of these arduous

journeys, poets have given voice to those who experience shifts of language and consciousness, spiritual deprivation and renewal, familial separation and reunion, and adaptation to being strangers in a strange land. André Aciman states, "Each one of us is a dislodged citizen of a country that was never really his, but that he has learned to long for and cannot forget. The fault lines of exile and diaspora always run deep, and we are always from elsewhere, and from elsewhere before that."

It's those aspects of elsewhere, physical and imagined, as well as the more concrete (literally and figuratively) aspects of the here and now, that the poets in this anthology explore and engage. More than one hundred poets from a wide range of cultural backgrounds deepen into personal stories of displacement, of migration and exile, and of past language and tradition set against the dissonances and unrecognizable rituals of cultures sometimes welcoming, often fearful or antagonistic. The process of (at times reluctant) assimilation is recorded in these poems through the smallest details, through the ordinary progressions of a life – its loves and labors – which take on significance as meanings of identity, of national and global citizenship, reconstruct themselves.

"How can we sing the songs of the Lord while in a foreign land?" asks the anonymous poet. The poets in this anthology attempt such songs, not only of the Lord in various guises, but also of themselves and their families, their loved ones past and present, their languages and lives, all toward defining, in more encompassing terms, migration as disruptive, wondrous, challenging, desperate, ecstatic, and – not least of all – reinventive.

Mihaela Moscaliuc
Michael Waters

CROSSINGS

OUTSIDE PLATO'S REPUBLIC, THE LAST POETS WAIT FOR DEPARTURE

Hong Kong International Airport, 1989

. . . *the poet himself is a China*
– Liu Hongbin, Chinese poet-in-exile

1

This one, tired from the long journey,
leans back in his airport chair. The stain of travel,
tattoo of sweat and the lips of sleeping women
pressed unknowingly to his shoulders mid-flight.
Not for love – no, but for rest. How their faces turned
inward the way a cat's pink tongue fills a wound
with an instinct for sweetness and iron.
Grounded, he is nothing now. A castoff map,
a blankness scarcely smudged by the sounding rings
of impinging continents. Land he has only seen
through mists. Has only witnessed in the fine print
at the bottom of passports and visas, the insides of cans,
the raised edges of boxes made somewhere else.
Somewhere forgettable. The sick and insane piecing
each plastic toy together, immune to pleasure.

2

In the corner, against the bullet-proof glass,
another raises his arms high above his head,
as if in prayer, or uttering a name to be nailed
like a piton into a hardened cliff face. This unbending
yearning. These barren limbs sprouting from a man
worn smooth by wind and water. How they stretch,
reaching for a heaven of silence, some dim realm
of rope and boards. A bridge. A strict metered offering.
Even. Still. The emptiness of fired clay. A scale.
A measure of wanting. Each hand a receptacle of
ghosts.

3

The last one traces the outbound curve
of an O that returns to its origin again,
stopping once before moving on. She thinks
of round coins punched through with squares,
the angle of characters lifted in relief, the thin
red string that holds them together around her neck.
O, she opens her mouth in a question wide enough
to hold a world the shape of her lips. O is the letter
she leaves at the gate for her lover, for the one
who is always nowhere, too late and too soon.

THE MIGRANT'S REPLY

We have been running for so long. We are tired. We
want to rest. We don't want
to wake up tomorrow and pack our bags. We have
gone 10,000 miles. We have
boarded a row boat, tug boat, bus, freight train. We
have a cell phone and some bread.

Our eyes are dry. Our breath needs washing. What
next? You are putting up
a wall on your Southern flank? What an irony. The
country that accepts refugees
does not want us. We qualify. We have scars and our
host governments hunted

at least some of us. The rest fled in fear. Gangs do not
spare even the children.
White vans took away our uncles, our cousins. Do you
think they have been made
into plowshares? Ay, what are you saying? Too easy.
Too easy to wear our hearts

in these words, in slings, on our faces, furrowed,
perplexed. What happened
to kindness to strangers? Why do we have to be
herded like prisoners, held

in a holding camp? We are human beings and, like
you, in safer countries,

we have the same obligation to save ourselves and our
children. Oh, the children.
Look at them. Give them food and school and a new
set of clothes. Give them
a chance. Whether you are red or blue the eye of the
hurricane does not

discriminate. We are your tumbling weeds, hurling
cars, flooding banks. And
we are diggers of the dykes. We can teach you so
many languages and visions.
You would learn so much: you would never ever say
lock us up.

From *THE GOLDEN VENTURE*

The freighter *Golden Venture* ran aground off Rockaway Beach, Queens in 1993, carrying nearly three hundred undocumented immigrants from China. Ten died trying to reach shore. Many were jailed for years in York, Pennsylvania as their asylum claims worked through the legal system. Those who were paroled are still without final legal status.

What Chen cannot say . . .

"I had been watching the mockingbirds
on the ledge outside all night
& given up thinking
I was like them with their prepositions
signaling they knew their way
in, around, above, over, with & through.

There was just me here alone
so when the jailer – shaking keys
like a baby's rattle – told me to go, I thought
just knowing the door was open was enough
but when he threatened to walk away
I said, *Yes, I am coming*, gathered my papers
my origami hands

so that he did not think I loved his
blue eyes so much to stay
& ran.

The door was like that.
When I thought it would not open & nothing
could be on the other side, it did
& when I think it will never close, there is
someone there saying, *Hurry up*.

Here is a flower I folded for you
when I thought I would not see you again
& here are my empty hands."

IMMIGRATION INTERVIEW WITH DON FRANCISCO

In the church was the deepest
well of the city where the priest
was lowered every morning.

[*Please say more*]

I've split open the small fish
and counted the candles tucked inside –
all the pink nails tapping the wicks.

[*Please elaborate*]

If I had children,
there would be no reason
to empty the bowls
stagnant with rain water –
no reason at all to keep saying
"you are almost."

[*Please say more*]

The wasps: their multitude of clapping hands.

[*Please elaborate*]

How small the dolls.
How insignificant
the hands that move them.

[*Please say more*]

Perhaps the butterflies are mute because
no one would believe their terrible stories.

IMMIGRATION AND NATURALIZATION SERVICE REPORT #46

for Javier O. Huerta

After the body was bagged and whisked away, we noticed a scarlet pelt on the sand. "This guy had it nice, sleeping on a pelt for days," Ignacio joked. He paused mid-laugh, bent down, ran his hand through the fur. One of his fingers snagged. "This isn't a pelt, it's a patch of wolf ears," he said. "No, they're too large," I replied. "Then they must be coyote ears," he murmured. Sweat gathered in the small of my back. "Ignacio, should we radio headquarters?" I asked. Two ears rose slowly from the patch. I said a few more words. Nothing. I uttered my own name. Two more ears unfurled. We stepped back from the patch, called out the names of our fathers and mothers. Ramón. Juana. Octavio. More and more ears rose. Rodolfo. Gloria . . .

EDUARDO C. CORRAL (1973 –)

THE PASSPORT

They don't recognize me in the shadows
That suck my color in this passport.
To them my wound is a showroom
For a tourist who passionately collects pictures.
They don't recognize me. Don't leave
The palm of my hand without a sun
Because the trees
Know me . . .
  The spinning mills of rain know me.
Don't leave me mummified like the moon!

The birds follow
The palm of my hand to the distant airport,
And all the wheat fields,
All the prisons,
All the pale sepulchres,
All the barbed boundaries,
All the waving handkerchiefs,
All the dark eyes,
All the eyes
Are with me, but the masters
Drop them from this passport!

Is it my name that brings dishonor? Or is it
My love for the land I raised in my hands?
Today Job cries the sky's fill:
   Don't make me a lesson twice!

True masters! Honorable prophets!
Don't ask the trees about their names.
Don't ask the wadis about their mothers.
From my forehead gushes the sword of light
And from my fingers flow rivers.
The heart of every man is my nationality;
So rid me of this passport.

WAVE
Song Lyrics

Wave goodbye
Everybody waves goodbye
Climb aboard the train
Turn and wave goodbye again

Some go north, some go south
Maybe east, some left out
Some are rich, some are poor
But everybody's got to wave

Wave goodbye
We're headed for the other side
The sun shines brighter there
And everyone's got golden hair.

They went north, they went south
Maybe east, some left out
Some are rich, some are poor
Someone blessed somewhat more

Because I'm sick
We're gonna find the ones that left
A boy climbs aboard the train
Never to wave bye again

They went north, they went south
Maybe east, some left out
Some are rich, some are poor
But everybody's got to wave

Don't you cry
We made it to the other side
The sun's not brighter here
It only shines on golden hair

I went north, I went south
Maybe east, some left out
Some are rich, some are poor
But everybody's got to wave

MAKING LIFE

> Jah never run no wire fence
> – Bob Marley

The cherry afterglow of Negril spring break,
sunset rays knit into his tam from the gold
ball dropped behind Rick's cafe,

my student oversteps a gray snowbank
on Liberty to ask me "Lorna, how can you
live in exile?"

Because it would take too long to tell
how I left because my Jamaica was like
a faceman lover

with too many other women he was seeing
on the side and I might have just died
waiting for him

to finally get round to doing right by me.
But that is too long a story, so I wander
and wonder instead:

is it because we came from a continent
why we can't settle on our islands?

Did our recrossing begin with deportation
of maroons to Liberia via Nova Scotia?

Are we all trying to work our way back
to Africa? For soon as we fought free

we the West Indians picked up foot
and set out over wide waters, to Cuba

and Panama, anywhere in the Americas.
And we never call ourselves exiles.

We see our sojournings as "making life."
So after world wars when they wanted

souls to bury dead and raise near-dead,
they called us in as duppy conquerors.

But when the job was done, they then
tried to exorcise our task force,

but we remained, took their brickbats
and became Blackbrits and Jamericans.

I first came north to paint pictures, but
maybe I wanted firsthand acquaintance

with the fanciful places named in songs.
Isle of Joy, the song said Manhattan was.

I'm from island in the sun, I had to come
and my sweetheart poetry joined me.

Not really exiled you see; just making life.

MAP OF KOREA, 1950

A map between them, father and daughter,
dishes cleared, his newspaper pushed aside –
she's home for the weekend; it's his birthday.
The line between the North – shown as mostly
white space – and the bustling South
is concise. So familiar, in fact, it's cliché.
What's the province where grandmother was born?
This is what she likes: ask and answer, glide
of her exhibit across the table,
each fact a new rock in her palm, that weight
of knowledge. Hamhung. The camps in Chungcheong.
The map is small. Because it lacks detail
he draws the Imjin lightly, in pencil –
wading, she'd strapped him in quilts to her back –
here a curl down the coast of the Yellow Sea.
This is what he likes: the pencil's lightness
in his hand, the clean new page, the kitchen lamp
simple as a moon above their table.

ANNIE KIM (1974–)

STONE

The best thing I did was
  move my body from one side of the world
to the other. This required a visa,
  which required a bribe.

The bribe, placed in the palm
  of a man with a gun,
took my mother's monthly wage packet.
  The man with a gun

let me speak to a clerk.
  He too wanted a wage
because it would be his job
  to have words with a judge

for another month's salary.
  The official wanted his bribe
so listened to the clerk
  escorted by the soldier as he held his gun.

As I sat with my mother
  on the steps of the court,
drinking soda, waiting
  for one man to say yes, my mother said,

"In Uganda a bribe stops men
    doing nothing. It rolls away the stone."
Her sips were slower than mine,
    each separated by this prayer.

From *THE IRAQI NIGHTS*

We cross borders lightly
like clouds.
Nothing carries us,
but as we move on
we carry rain,
and an accent,
and a memory
of another place.

IN THE HOLD

After an unmeasured time as a stowaway
in the stifling void, listening to the waves,
the rats, the grains of wheat settling,
my father heard church bells
and knew he'd come to port.
When they rang past twelve
he was sure the war had broken out,
the world war that had been expected
all through childhood, for so long
tailors adjusted their chalk lines for it,
painters shaded it into the middle distance
like an unknown primary, preachers exhausted
the endings for their sermons;
now my father in the dark cubbyhole
that might be endless, or just a hair
larger than his ungrown body,
counts the coins in his sack,
the stitches in the gunny weave –
he takes his pulse, then having
no more real things, he counts
the members of his family, the chimneys
of his village, all the days
of his life in the old country.

D. NURKSE (1949–)

ADRIFT

> A shipping container of rubber duckies made in China for the US washed overboard in 1992, and some of them traveled and washed ashore over 17,000 miles over 15 years.

Let's go ahead and assume it's yellow.
What little of science I know:
its plastic skin invincible against salt water,
but not the sun –
we can only ask so much.
Will it fade or brown?
What I mean to say is
I would want one of these
for my daughter:
its internal clock set to the mercy of the currents
that have been predictable for centuries,
but mercy is not the word anyone
would choose.
Sometimes not making sense and floating
are the same.
Each wave is its own beginning and ending.
Through international waters,
you could have caused an incident:
no one knowing you,
never reaching the hands that hoped for you.

Rough immigrant, or
free refugee –
floating flagless,
fading border,
stamped with words but not your name.

MIGRANT STORIES

Our landlord Captain Niko tells us how
his ancestors landed on this island
two centuries ago.

Each migrant chose
a stone and threw it deep into the fog.
Where it landed each one built a house.

The Greeks in Uruguay, he says, once exchanged
shoes they made from the skin of unborn calves
for feta cheese and olives – Greek essentials –

and told him of a kinsman there who wanted
to return back home. A bride was waiting.
But bandits stole his money; shamed, he fled

to the interior. This morning the Captain
is carrying a broken oar up from the sea,
torn life-vests. Looking at us. No stories now.

POLITICAL REFUGEE, ONE MONTH ON

What he's lost isn't the uninterrupted sun
or the jokey patois of his friends, their fingers fanned
to brace the passed jug as they bantered, full
of idiom and pun, after long meetings.

He's lost himself, the one he was at home,
the last to leave the plane, clutched to his seat
for fear his blood would freeze (the ground outside
white with flakes, they said, of frozen water).

When they led him out, shivering in his short-sleeved
shirt,
a blanket pressed on his shoulders, to his plump hosts
whose mouths curved around strange syllables
of welcome, to the donated coat, to the land of ever-

after, he called himself survivor, snatched
from the tribe of the dead; but now he counts himself
not saved but strayed, estranged and numb, a beast
in the field, wheeling for direction, knowing none.

PICTURE BRIDE

She was a year younger
than I,
twenty-three when she left Korea.
Did she simply close
the door of her father's house
and walk away. And
was it a long way
through the tailor shops of Pusan
to the wharf where the boat
waited to take her to an island
whose name she had
only recently learned,
on whose shore
a man waited,
turning her photograph
to the light when the lanterns
in the camp outside
Waialua Sugar Mill were lit
and the inside of his room
grew luminous
from the wings of moths
migrating out of the cane stalks?
What things did my grandmother
take with her? And when
she arrived to look

into the face of the stranger
who was her husband,
thirteen years older than she,
did she politely untie
the silk bow of her jacket,
her tent-shaped dress
filling with the dry wind
that blew from the surrounding fields
where the men were burning the cane?

CATHY SONG (1955–)

DEPARTURE

A liner in its fiery berth
Burns away the chains of earth.

The thousand emigrants have but one small
Accordion among them all.

The anchor's hoisted, on each arm
A mermaid wriggles with alarm,

Jumps back into the ocean, so astounded,
She's not aware of being wounded.

The ocean's voices high and higher
Swell, illuminating our desire.

The seagulls flurry to and fro
To wave us on, and on we go.

The high seas come on board, disguised
As blind men with briny eyes.

And in the gulf of space, at last
They slowly climb the mizzenmast.

 JULES SUPERVIELLE (1884–1960)
TRANSLATED BY JAMES KIRKUP

TRANSMIGRATION

Spirit, when I flee this jungle, you must too.
I will take our silver bars, necklace dowry, and the
kettle
forged from metal scraps just after the last monsoon.

Among the foliage, we must be ready to see
the half-decayed. You must not run off no matter how
much
flesh you smell.

Nor should you wander to chase an old mate.

Spirit, we are in this with each other the way the
night geese
in migration need the stars.

When I make the crossing, you must not be taken no
matter what
the current gives. When we reach the camp,

there will be thousands like us.
If I make it onto the plane, you must follow me to the
roads
and waiting pastures of America.

We will not ride the water today on the shoulders of
buffalo
as we used to many years ago, nor will we forage
for the sweetest mangoes.

I am refugee. You are too. Cry, but do not weep.

We walk out the door.

REFUGEES

Bent under burdens which sometimes
can be seen and sometimes can't,
they trudge through mud or desert sands,
hunched, hungry,

silent men in heavy jackets,
dressed for all four seasons,
old women with crumpled faces,
clutching something – a child, the family
lamp, the last loaf of bread?

It could be Bosnia today,
Poland in September '39, France
eight months later, Germany in '45,
Somalia, Afghanistan, Egypt.

There's always a wagon or at least a wheelbarrow
full of treasures (a quilt, a silver cup,
the fading scent of home),
a car out of gas marooned in a ditch,
a horse (soon left behind), snow, a lot of snow,
too much snow, too much sun, too much rain,

and always that special slouch
as if leaning toward another, better planet,

with less ambitious generals,
less snow, less wind, fewer cannons,
less History (alas, there's no
such planet, just that slouch).

Shuffling their feet,
they move slowly, very slowly
toward the country of nowhere,
and the city of no one
on the river of never.

 ADAM ZAGAJEWSKI (1945–)
TRANSLATED BY CLARE CAVANAGH

PROMISED LAND

THE EMBODIMENT

since spider feel at home
with thread and rope

I thought I'd try Eu-rope
(the name sounded promising)

so I headed for England
land of hope and unfinished glory
like Schubert's symphony

leaving Amsterdam to Surinam spinners
and Paris to Martinique weavers

arrived at Heathrow not quite light
eight nothing-to-declare suitcases
balanced on eight metropolis-dreaming legs

soon got used to juggling eight cups of tea
like I was spider embodiment of Earl Grey

and nobody made any comment
till I metamorphosed into proper
tophat ascot gent

and bought a piece
of property in Kent

then the pauses
became pregnant

and I heard myself say

No I'm not on holiday
Spider is here to stay

OF IT ALL

for Anthony Lacavaro

I say *This, after all, is the trick of it all*
when suddenly you say "Arabic of it all."

After Algebra there was Geometry – and then
Calculus –
But I'd already failed the arithmetic of it all.

White men across the U.S. love their wives' curries –
I say *O No!* to the turmeric of it all.

"Suicide represents . . . a privileged moment. . . ."
Then what keeps you – and me – from being sick of
it all?

The telephones work, but I'm still cut off from you.
We star in *America*, fast epic of it all.

What shapes galaxies and keeps them from flying
apart?
There's that missing mass, the black magic of it all.

What makes yours the rarest edition is just this:
it's bound in human skin, final fabric of it all.

I'm smashed, fine Enemy, in your isolate mirror.
Why the diamond display then – in public – of it all?

Before the palaver ends, hear the sparrows' songs,
the quick quick quick, O the quick of it all.

For the suicidally beautiful, autumn now starts.
Their fathers' heroes, boys gallop, kick off it all.

The sudden storm swept its ice across the great
    plains.
How did you find me, then, in the thick of it all?

Across the world one aches for New York, but to long
for New York in New York's most tragic of it all.

For Shahid too the night went "quickly as it came" –
After that, old friend, came the music of it all.

FIRES BURN IN BRADFORD, ROCKSTONE FLING INNAH OLDHAM

I don't see no Asians on the football pitch,
A mus a dem turn fi seh "Inglan is a bitch"
Fire burn a Bradford, Rockstone fling inna Oldham,
But a who dem a blame? the one Indian.

The one thing the camera never sees
Like a petrol to a match the b.n.p.
Gathering momentum and versatility

> Propaganda leaves,
> Brutality trunk tree,
> Wolves in sheep's clothing
> Hiding underground,
> u.k. terrorist network,
> man from out of town.

But a di Indian youth we see angry on t.v.
Kickin up a rumpus in their own high street
A gallery of brown faces, dem did get the blame
Can't speak our language Oh what a shame!

Remind me . . .
we must give them some money to enrich their
    community.

How many years to the next election, one two
    or three?
A few new parks . . . photographed . . . skylarks,
Between politicians and shop owners.

The same ones who disown us?

20 years time Asians may be partly accepted
Is then the Eastern Bloc migrants
will be targeted and rejected.

58 DREADLOCK ALIEN (RICHARD GRANT) (DATES N/A)

RURAL SCENE

The luminous Norfolk skies,
the tractors, the gunshots,
the still ponds, the darting rabbits,
cow parsley by the field gates –

all are re-imagining themselves
because Tariq walks in his village,
part of the scene, yet conspicuous,
as if he is walking a tiger.

MONIZA ALVI (1954–)

THE DAUGHTERS

My daughters have lost
two hundred and thirty-six teeth
and counting.
They possess so many skills: they can
craft sophisticated weaponry such as blow-pipes,
lances and slings and know what the sharp end
of a peacock's feather is for.
Last month they constructed a canoe
and saved the *Purdu Mephistopheles* from extinction.
They may not know that a bird in the hand
is worth noting but have learned
never to bleed on any of the auspicious days
and are aware that pleasure
is a point on a continuum.
I fear they will never make good brides,
they are too fond of elliptical constructions
and are prone to lying in the dirt reading
paragraphs in the clouds.
Their shadows are long.
They know many things, my girls;
when they are older I will teach them
that abundance and vulcanisation
are bad words.
When they sleep, they sleep heavy;
I go into their rooms and check their teeth.

TOWN GOSSIP
Indiana, 1994

But we were strange girls, girls thrown together
in mismatched clothes, shaved wisps of sideburns, that
    Arab last name.

My father got letters: *Please don't drop the girls off early.*
There's no one here to watch them.

Kids asked, *What do you mean, your mom's not here?*
  Wolves without her –

unkempt in the eyes of our teachers
– *Sarah hoards the week's lunch money in her desk*

because she is too scared
to hand it to the cafeteria cashier.

Those days we'd ride our bikes down Highway 1
to the hotel where our mother last stayed

and we'd loop the lot for hours, sawing paths between
    the bumpers
for no reason other than that door was briefly hers.

Our guidance counselor
is excellent with children from divorced families.

We stole the bitten-eared tabby
from the neighbors,

mined playground rocks,
pocketed Mom's old lipstick tubes.

Mariam is outspoken in class, but we worry her peers make fun
of her alopecia. She spends recess on the blacktop next to her teacher.

Leaf-strung crabapple girls. We climbed the arthritic tree
outside our dentist's office, clutched there until sundown.

Ruth wears men's overcoats to school.
Do they belong to you?

ROOMSEEKER IN LONDON

I saw him rapping her door
Field man of old empire stood
  with that era he brought

She knew a man from sunny skies
She knew a bundle in arms
  that walked with a hopeful mind

This then was the trial

Sugar man sighed
  on outrage the lady effused
  and she quickly bolted in

His knocks hurt both ways
Can two poles consummate
  sky and earth and blood?

The man wondered
How many more doors
  would his gesture take?

MY REDISCOVERED LAND

I lost my land
on a day of loud alarm
on a day of tears and bitter sorrow

I found my land again
and took the orphan to heart.
To make her fruitful
I planted trees
along her pathways
renewed her green spaces
to her beauties
added numerous flowers
also a lake
with brimming water

I rediscovered my land
I walk there without sheltering.

 ANDRÉE CHEDID (1920–2011)
TRANSLATED BY KATHRYN KIMBALL

HOME

These days whenever I stay away too long,
anything I happen to clap eyes on,
(that red telephone box) somehow makes me
miss here more than anything I can name.

My heart performs a jazzy drum solo
when the crow's feet on the 747
scrape down at Heathrow. H.M. Customs . . .
I resign to the usual inquisition,

telling me with Surrey loam caked
on the tongue, home is always elsewhere.
I take it like an English middleweight
with a questionable chin, knowing

my passport photo's too open-faced,
haircut wrong (an afro) for the decade;
the stamp, British Citizen not bold enough
for my liking and too much for theirs.

The cockney cab driver begins chirpily
but can't or won't steer clear of race,
so rounds on Asians. I lock eyes with him
in the rearview when I say I live with one.

He settles at the wheel grudgingly,
in a huffed silence. Cha! Drive man!
I have legal tender burning in my pocket
to move on, like a cross in Transylvania.

At my front door, why doesn't the lock
recognise me and budge? I give an extra
twist and fall forward over the threshold
piled with the felicitations of junk mail,

into a cool reception in the hall.
Grey light and close skies I love you.
Chokey streets, roundabouts and streetlamps
with tyres chucked round them, I love you.

Police officer, your boots need re-heeling.
Robin Redbreast, special request – a burst
of song so the worm can wind to the surface.
We must all sing for our suppers or else.

WHEN I FIRST SAW SNOW

Tarrytown, N.Y.

Bing Crosby was singing "White Christmas"
on the radio, we were staying at my aunt's house
waiting for papers, my father was looking for a job.
We had trimmed the tree the night before,
sap had run on my fingers and for the first time
I was smelling pine wherever I went.
Anais, my cousin, was upstairs in her room
listening to Danny and the Juniors.
Haigo was playing Monopoly with Lucy, his sister,
Buzzy, the boy next door, had eyes for her
and there was a rattle of dice, a shuffling
of Boardwalk, Park Place, Marvin Gardens.
There were red bows on the Christmas tree.
It had snowed all night.
My boot buckles were clinking like small bells
as I thumped to the door and out
onto the grey planks of the porch dusted with
snow.
The world was immaculate, new,
even the trees had changed color,
and when I touched the snow on the railing
I didn't know what I had touched, ice or fire.
I heard, "I'm dreaming . . ."
I heard, "At the hop, hop, hop . . . oh, baby."

I heard "B & O" and the train in my imagination
  was whistling through the great plains.
And I was stepping off,
I was falling deeply into America.

From *LARA*

Liverpool, England, 1949 –

TAIWO

OH MAMA! Your pride when I boarded the *Apapa*.
Your son, a man now, riding the whale to paradise!

Remember the man's voice from Broadcasting House
calling us over the air waves from England?

"London calling The Empire! Calling The Empire!
Come in Nigeria!" *I'm coming! I'm coming!*

I shouted at night into the warm winds on deck.
Mama, my dreams have been my fuel for years,

all those British films for sixpence at the movie house.
See London, then die! I was desperate to get here!

When I finally landed in Liverpool it was Heaven,
I had hoped for snow but it was just very cold.

These people run everywhere and wear mufflers.
Older cousin Sam came to greet me at the docks,

just as well because I thought the fast automobiles
would kill me. I asked Sam if many people are killed

by cars. He laughed, "You will get used to life here."
The Africans have European wives and sailor's
children.

Sam has a house in Princess Park in Toxteth district,
his wife Maureen is Irish and their six-year-old

daughter is Beatrice. I said, "Why a white wife, Sam?"
He replied, "When in Rome do as the Romans do."

Mama, I will write a letter soon. I promise you.

SAM SAYS this country is like fisherman's bait, Mama.
It attracts, you bite, then you are trapped. I told him

I'd be here five years, get my degree and leave.
Tomorrow I head for London. Centre of the Empire!

Sam drinks stout every night complaining that
John Bull
only gives him work on the railways, and I've met
elders

in the Yoruba Club in Croxteth Street who came
in the last century as stowaways or seamen,

fought in two world wars for Britain, but believe
back home is paradise. I argue Nigeria is small time.

Why eat rice and stew when you can taste Yorkshire
pud, meat and two veg. You can buy anything here,

there are so many shops, pubs on every street corner
and houses have all the modern conveniences.

Many people are respectful but some idiots shout
"Oi! Johnny! Sambo! Darkie! Nigger!" at us.

The elders tell us to take no nonsense from them,
so if I am abused I say quietly, "Just call me Taiwo,"

and boof! I fight them. Even the West Indians say
"Do you people still live in trees in the bush?"

Mama, in this country I am coloured.
Back home I was just me.

ANISE SEED

The plant had been dried & beaten to make the
seeds fall

She brought a jarful from the old country

There would be holiday cookies & anisette liqueur

There would be a back yard for growing fragrant
herbs

After her husband died the jar sat unopened on a shelf

One day I asked my mother if those seeds hadn't
dried out

One day looking as if she were in a hurry

She wrapped a few kernels into the dirt behind
my house

Then rocked back & forward

Heart-shaped leaves in spring

Explosion of white flowers in July

Condiment for soups & stews

Tea to soothe my crying babies

Oil to rub on my mother's knees after radiation

Wash for red & swollen eyes

My mother's hand has vanished but is active

Just so, you come to wake me anise seed

As I do the most American thing there is

Eat lunch alone

Today it's pea, fava & stalks of anise soup

WAS FEDERICO GARCÍA LORCA LONELY IN NEW YORK?

Was Federico García Lorca lonely in New York?
Did he climb the streets like a statue of rock
rebelling against the sculptor, turning on
his creator to take the chisel out of his hands?

Was Federico crying in New York?
Did he wipe his tears with hands holding oranges
whose juice punishes all men of crippled hope,
or did he stare at the harbor and wait for the gulls
to screech into blinding stars shooting across
immigration lines, bread lines of people
too hungry to drink their cups of blood?

Was García Lorca able to sleep in New York?
Did he wake above the city blocks to identify
the makers of brick and mortar, builders of slums,
ghosts of crowded rooms, doors of troubled sleep?

Did Lorca slash the duende in New York?
Did he find the black guitar in the ashes
raining over the Brooklyn Bridge,
or meet the many-colored gypsy in the alley
of singing flames, the barrio of wailing love
and the forgotten tambourine?

Was Federico searching for something in New York?
Did Spain turn into a wolf hunting for him
as he looked for the woman of flowers in Central Park,
search for the child in the fish markets of Harlem,
go after the crowds of people everywhere?

Did García Lorca go crazy in New York?
Were his eyes drilling the heart of the subways
to find a place to hide his poems?
Before leaving, did he dance the steps of death
in recognition of firing squads lining up?

Did Lorca run toward the lights
of the harbor of false liberty?
Did he finally get out of the way,
or was he carried to the moon by the thousands
of pigeons fleeing the future city?

LLAMAS, CWMPENGRAIG

Oh you – coming to greet us over the farm-gate
Your camel-like heads elegant against this Welsh
  hilltop
Whose sheep graze like commoners beneath your
  gaze

Your heads turn as one,
Ears – inverted commas, sickles, sweet horns of plenty
Eyes languid behind fringed yashmak of lashes

Peru seems a long way off,
As does Guyana; but for a moment there we shared
An echo between us, of continents.

A SNAPSHOT OF MY FATHER, 1928

His hick tie
flares out into the granular wind,
his thick kraut hair sprouts from under a cap you
wouldn't be caught dead in,

but he's smiling, he's
holding hard to the ship's rail,
and he won't let go because he's on his way now,
he's on his way to America,

a country he smelled
when the North Sea warmed to summer,
a country he saw when the story in a reader said
river, trees, land, money.

So he's eighteen, and somehow
he's on his way now. The Atlantic wind
blows his baggy trousers way out in front of him,
and he looks like famine,

this hayseed
with bad teeth, this carpenter
sporting a jacket patched at an elbow, this Dutchman
wearing a new life in his eyes.

But he doesn't know
what he looks like, or doesn't care,
but just cares to hold tight to the rail because
everything will be all right,

he's on his way now,
my father, for richer or poorer,
smiling for fifty years now because he's going to
make it
to America.

THE PINEAPPLE TREE

In leaving Palestine, he wanted to find in these lands a pineapple tree. He dreamed of a leafy green tree like the one God placed in paradise.

He abandoned his country with the hope of a new one and didn't find what he wished for.

In this poem, my grandfather can pick pineapples from the crown of a tree because in a poem trees that don't exist can actually grow, as can their millennial fruits and even a country of birth.

However, I insist, what I want to sprout is not the tree, but the belief there is still a place where pineapple trees abound.

ROLANDO KATTAN (1979–)
TRANSLATED BY NICOLETTE REIM

FOR THE KOREAN GRANDMOTHER ON SUNSET BOULEVARD

So you are here. Night comes as it does
elsewhere: light pulls slowly away
from telephone posts, shadows of buildings
darken the pavement like something
spilled. Even the broken moon
seems to turn its face.
And again you find yourself
on this dark riverbed, this asphalt
miracle, holding your end of a rope
that goes slack when you tug it.
Such grief you bear alone.
But wait. Just now a light
approaches, its rich band draws
you forward, out of shadow.
It is here, the bus that will ferry
you home. Go ahead,
grandmother, go on.

AMERÍCAN

we gave birth to a new generation,
AmeRícan, broader than lost gold
never touched, hidden inside the
puerto rican mountains.

we gave birth to a new generation,
AmeRícan, it includes everything
imaginable you-name-it-we-got-it
society.

we gave birth to a new generation,
AmeRícan salutes all folklores,
european, indian, black, spanish,
and anything else compatible:

AmeRícan, singing to composer pedro flores' palm
trees high up in the universal sky!

AmeRícan, sweet soft spanish danzas gypsies
moving lyrics la *española* cascabelling
presence always singing at our side!

AmeRícan, beating jíbaro modern troubadours
crying guitars romantic continental
bolero love songs!

AmeRícan, across forth and across back
back across and forth back
forth across and back and forth
our trips are walking bridges!

it all dissolved into itself, the attempt
was truly made, the attempt was truly
absorbed, digested, we spit out
the poison, we spit out the malice,
we stand, affirmative in action,
to reproduce a broader answer to the
marginality that gobbled us up abruptly!

AmeRícan, walking plena-rhythms in new york,
strutting beautifully alert, alive,
many turning eyes wondering,
admiring!

AmeRícan, defining myself my own way any way many
ways Am e Rícan, with the big R and the
accent on the í!

AmeRícan, like the soul gliding talk of gospel
boogie music!

AmeRícan, speaking new words in spanglish tenements,
fast tongue moving street corner *"que*
corta" talk being invented at the insistence
of a smile!

AmeRícan, abounding inside so many ethnic english
people, and out of humanity, we blend
and mix all that is good!

AmeRícan, integrating in new york and defining our
own *destino*, our own way of life,

AmeRícan, defining the new america, humane america,
admired america, loved america, harmonious
america, the world in peace, our energies
collectively invested to find other civili-
zations, to touch God, further and further,
to dwell in the spirit of divinity!

AmeRícan, yes, for now, for i love this, my second
land, and i dream to take the accent from
the altercation, and be proud to call
myself american, in the u.s. sense of the
word, AmeRícan, America!

AFTER CELEBRATING OUR ASYLUM STORIES AT WEST YORKSHIRE PLAYHOUSE, LEEDS

So, define her separately,
She's not just another
Castaway washed up your
Rough seas like driftwood,
It's the nameless battles
Your sages burdened her
People that broke her back;
Define him differently,
He's not another squirrel
Ousted from your poplars,
It's the endless cyclones,
Earthquakes, volcanoes,
Floods, mud and dust that
Drafted him here; define
Them warmly, how could
Your economic émigré queue
At your job centres day after
Day? If you must, define us
Gently, how do you hope
To see the tales we bear
When you refuse to hear
The whispers we share?

THE ONLY THING FAR AWAY

In this country, Jamaica is not quite as far
as you might think. Walking through Peckham
in London, West Moss Road in Manchester,
you pass green and yellow shops
where tie-headwomen bargain over the price
of dasheen. And beside Jamaica is Spain
selling large yellow peppers, lemon to squeeze
onto chicken. Beside Spain is Pakistan, then Egypt,
Singapore, the world . . . here, strangers build home
together, flood the ports with curry and papayas;
in Peckham and on Moss Road, the place smells
of more than just patty or tandoori. It smells like
Mumbai, like the Castries, like Princess Street, Jamaica.
Sometimes in this country, the only thing far away
is this country.

FISHBONE

At dinner, my mother says if one gets stuck
in your throat, roll some rice into a ball
and swallow it whole. She says things
like this and the next thing out of her mouth

is *did you know Madonna is pregnant?*
But I want to ponder the basket of fried smelt
on the table, lined with paper towels to catch
the grease – want to study their eyes

like flat soda, wonder how I'm supposed
to eat them whole. Wonder why we can't
have normal food for breakfast like at Sara's house –
Cheerios, or sometimes if her mother is home:

buttered toast and soft-boiled eggs
in her grandmother's dainty blue egg cups
and matching blue spoon. Safe. Pretty.
Nothing with eyes. Under the flakes of fried crust,

I see a shimmer of skin as silver as foil,
like the dimes my mother tapes to a board
for each year I'm alive. How she tucked this
into my suitcase before I left for college

and I forgot about '93 *and* '95. How she said
she'll never find a '93, and shouldn't this
be a great thing to one day put into an oak frame,
but not now, not until we find the missing coin?

How we don't have many traditions left, thanks
to Your Father. These are the things she says
instead of a blessing to our food. These are the words
that stick inside me as I snap off the next head.

THE PRAYER LABYRINTH

She went looking for her daughter. How many
visit Hades and live? Your only hope
is the long labyrinth of Visa Application
interviews with a volunteer from a charity
you're not allowed to meet. You've been caught:
by a knock on the door at dawn
or hiding in a truck of toilet tissue
or just getting stuck in a turn-stile.

You're on Dead Island: the Detention Centre.
The Russian refugees who leaped from the fifteenth
floor
of a Glasgow tower block to the Red Road
Springburn – Serge, Tatiana and their son,
who when the Immigration officers
were at the door, tied themselves together
before they jumped – knew what was coming.

Anyway you're here. Evidence of cigarette
burns all over your body has been dismissed
by the latest technology. You're dragged
from your room, denied medication
or a voice. You can't see your children,
they're behind bars somewhere else.

You go on hunger strike. You're locked
in a corridor for three days without water
then handcuffed through the biopsy
on your right breast. You've no choice
but to pray; and to walk the never-ending path
of meditation on *not yet.* Your nightmare
was home-grown; you're seeking sanctuary.
They say you don't belong. They give you
a broken finger, a punctured lung.

MY INDIA

India has moved in next door
She had flown in from Heathrow
Landed here at Number Ten
I am number nine. She has brought with her only her custom
And pocket book to declare
There is stress, goody goody
Damn, as in damn right
Cleavage look! As in sexy
But still no translation
For privacy or eating alone no solitude or wow, exclamation

Me, I fly infrequently
In the back bedroom at night
Rest in yesterday's reservoir drop off the ballast of this pen
Curl up asleep on paper cuttings:
There words will join up in dreams

This Ikea lucky bamboo only 99p
Durga announces from her hallway
I smile and close my door
Seal a distant railway sound
And in this silent Scotland
I hear a language all my own.

MIDNIGHT IN THE FOREIGN FOOD AISLE

Dear Uncle, is everything you love foreign
or are you foreign to everything you love?
We're all animals and the body wants what it wants,
I know. The blonde said *Come in, take off*
your coat and what do you want to drink?
Love is not haram, but after years of fucking
women who cannot pronounce your name,
you find yourself in the foreign food aisle,
beside the turmeric and the saffron of mothers' hands,
pressing your face into the ground, praying
in a language you haven't used in years.

WARSAN SHIRE (1988–)

EXPLORERS

They arrive inside
The object at evening.
There's no one to greet them.

The lamps they carry
Cast their shadows
Back into their own minds.

They write in their journals:

The sky and the earth
Are of the same impenetrable color.
If there are rivers and lakes,
They must be under the ground.
Of the marvels we sought, no trace.
Of the strange new stars, nothing.
There's not even wind or dust,
So we must conclude that someone
Passed recently with a broom . . .

As they write, the new world
Gradually stitches
Its black thread into them.

Eventually nothing is left
Except a low whisper
Which might belong
Either to one of them
Or to someone who came before.

It says: "I'm happy
We are finally all here . . .

Let's make this our home."

SOUTHERN CONE

I wept with my grandmother when Reagan
was shot because that's what she wanted.
At night, she'd tell me about a city built
by Evita for children in Buenos Aires, the city
of her first exile. Children went about
municipal duties in the small post office
and mini city hall to learn to be good citizens.
In Argentina she sold bread pudding
and gave French and English lessons from her
home for money to buy shoes. She promised
we'd go someday, but we never did. She'd say
Peruvians were gossipy, Argentinians snobbish, but
Chileans were above reproach. A little bit migrant,
a little bit food insecurity, she was the brass bust
of JFK on her altar, the holy card of Saint Anthony
on her TV. She was her green card and the ebony cross
above her bed. The lilted yes when she answered
the phone, and the song she liked to hum about bells
and God that ended tirin-tin-tin-tirin-tin-tan: miles
and ages away from her story, she sang it.

I let you go down to the little cellar because you were good.
This coffee is good! like mine   like tar   give me some
chocolate
I let you go down to the golden onions
to teach you tears can be sweet

Did we burn coal and breathe it day & night?
Did our rags turn black?

I have rags of every color – [laughs]
Ivory from bleaching   red & brown from bleedings
Green from garden   black from coughing

In the holloh house I looked down through cracks
in the boards and saw yellow water running from the
mines
When rains came
yellow water could wash us all away –

POEM WRITTEN FROM A SINGLE SNAPSHOT

On the beach in Monrovia,
my children and I are building sandcastles.
You can see the Atlantic's waves in the distance,
fighting for a place to roll their way onto shore.
Waves are flapping in the wind
as the tide rises up and down.
Before we know it, we are in the middle of water.
Besie is two years old. MT, who is only
six months, clings a short arm around my knee.
He's staring at Besie and the sandcastle
she's erecting with her right foot.
This is how my mother taught me
to build a sandcastle.
You put your foot down
and build mounds around it until
the castle becomes stable.
This is how we search for home.
You put your foot down in a place long enough
that new place becomes home.

NATURALIZATION

His tongue shorn, father confuses
snacks for snakes, kitchen for chicken.
It is 1992. Weekends, we paw at cheap
silverware at yard sales. I am told by mother
to keep our telephone number close,
my beaded coin purse closer. I do this.
The years are slow to pass, heavy-footed.
Because the visits are frequent, we memorize
shame's numbing stench. I nurse nosebleeds,
run up and down stairways, chew the wind.
Such were the times. All of us nearsighted.
Grandmother prays for fortune
to keep us around and on a short leash.
The new country is ill-fitting, lined
with cheap polyester, soiled at the sleeves.

JENNY XIE (1986–)

MOTHERLAND

DEAR MASOOM

We are happy to hear
you have electric in your home,
that the pipes by each window
keep you warm. What a kind
government to provide
milk, butter, and cheese.
Arey, if only ours would do the same –
but it can't keep the trash
off the capital's streets.
We hope you and Shilpa are well.
The little ones, send them
our love. Please come home soon.
Appa would like to see you
before she dies.

The blankets you mailed
are quite fine – Maya and I share
one, as I gave mine
to Appa. She coughs and rasps
all night despite the ginger tea.
I can hardly sleep
for the noise. Appa is growing older,
you know, so the monsoons make her
wheeze, the dust makes her wheeze,
weather changes make her wheeze.

I hear her now as I sit
wrapped in the one blanket
Maya and I share.

Brother, we are well
in most regards. We are keeping
warm in the sweaters you mailed
last year, the dry season upon us
already. At night the chill could break
your bones. Just last week
the *shim* vine's beans grew as shiny
as eggplant, but now the jinn
rise in the fields.

URSA MAJOR

dear mother in the sky
unbuckle the book

and erase all
the annotations

you could suckle or
suffocate me

how will you find
the little polar star in

the vast sky disowned
from his constellation

blinking at you across
unspeakable distance

KAZIM ALI (1971–)

CHEST

The outward form
weighs 125 pounds,

cherry skin
scarred by the sun:

    age spots, knots,
    a darkening figure.

Inside the dead
people live.

Gauze of green
nightgowns.

Mirage of black
and white marriages,

    their glue become
    a yellowed crust

    bubbling beneath
    plastic sheets.

The dead want to rise
from their acid bath.

The dead in shoeboxes,
hatboxes, passports.

The used
and the stamped.

Decades decaying
in tissue paper.

Relentless –
save the rot.

You can save
no one.

The bloodline
blown.

This heaving
heavy empty.

Unpack the casket
of history then

descend
into its red sea.

From *GUANAHANI*

like the beginnings – o odales o adagios – of islands
from under the clouds where I write the first poem

its brown warmth now that we recognize them
even from this thunder's distance

still w/out sound. so much hope
now around the heart of lightning that I begin to weep

w/such happiness of familiar landscap
such genius of colour. shape of bay. headland

the dark moors of the mountain
ranges. a door opening in the sky

right down into these new blues & sleeping yellows
greens – like a mother's

embrace like a lover's
enclosure. like schools

of fish migrating towards homeland. into the bright
light of xpectation. birth

of these long roads along the edge of Eleuthera,
now sinking into its memory behind us

MY VOICE

To cure myself of wanting Cuban songs,
I wrote a Cuban song about the need
For people to suppress their fantasies,
Especially unhealthy ones. The song
Began by making reference to the sea,
Because the sea is like a need so great
And deep it never can be swallowed. Then
The song explores some common myths
About the Cuban people and their folklore:
The story of a little Carib boy
Mistakenly abandoned to the sea;
The legend of a bird who wanted song
So desperately he gave up flight; a queen
Whose strength was greater than a rival king's.
The song goes on about morality,
And then there is a line about the sea,
How deep it is, how many creatures need
Its nourishment, how beautiful it is
To need. The song is ending now, because
I cannot bear to hear it any longer.
I call this song of needful love my voice.

RAFAEL CAMPO (1964–)

HOW TO CUT A POMEGRANATE

"Never," said my father,
"Never cut a pomegranate
through the heart. It will weep blood.
Treat it delicately, with respect.

Just slit the upper skin across four quarters.
This is a magic fruit,
so when you split it open, be prepared
for the jewels of the world to tumble out,
more precious than garnets,
more lustrous than rubies,
lit as if from inside.
Each jewel contains a living seed.
Separate one crystal.
Hold it up to catch the light.
Inside is a whole universe.
No common jewel can give you this."

Afterwards, I tried to make necklaces
of pomegranate seeds.
The juice spurted out, bright crimson,
and stained my fingers, then my mouth.

I didn't mind. The juice tasted of gardens
I had never seen, voluptuous
with myrtle, lemon, jasmine,
and alive with parrots' wings.

The pomegranate reminded me
that somewhere I had another home.

THE FIG EATERS, FIFTH ESTRANGEMENT

& there was the beauty of one sister
who was wild once, though you
will not believe or see, at first,
how she drew dark in the sun
& grew the blackest hairs
in the back of her house
where she climbed the trees
barefoot, the ten tiny toenails gleaming
like newborn, would-be claws,
& her shyness before us, the older two,
made her silent yet she climbed
& climbed, swiftly, roundly, happily,
as a way of speaking & showing what
she knew to do & loved, into
the tree's green & yellow head
to pluck the slow jewels of the fig eaters
from their habitat, those bugs whose mouths
were made only to eat what is soft
already, what is worn with rot, & whose mouths,
for we were not among the hunters,
had not evolved to hurt us, & the sister,
catching them with her hands, coaxing
them to ride her arms & hair before
toward us they rose out of the talon,

which did not know it was a talon,
in the new garden of our father's house
which was not the first garden, but the second,
paradise without dangers, as it should be, at least
in the beginning, where, in the narrow kitchen,
behind the strangely groomed bushes
cut into the shapes of spheres & animals,
never sat a bowl of figs I would have washed
for him if this had also been my wilderness
for they, the figs, were never saved,
& really, really we knew already that all the garden
could grow was the small girl & the world of beetles.
The heavy heart-sacs of the figs looted outside of
    the house,
whose purple cerebra heaved
with a familiar strain of starlight (ours), whose
plural green deaths fed the beetles &,
thusly, the sister, too, who,
in the absence of "real" siblings,
inherited the father & the yard, not greedily,
but truly, which made me stop
thinking, then, of our father's grief
in our absence from his country & his custody &
    house.
The plates & cups now used again.
The closets now filled with small & empty shoes.
There was relief to know

we were no longer the only ones for whom
he'd weep, though this, too, was our trouble, our
wound.

THE COUNTRY I FLEE FROM DAILY

It is the only tendriled
country in the world.
Its needy limbs reaching for miles
pulling me back into its despair.

It has so many little voices
announcing the annual revolutions,
the catastrophes of each month,
misery weekly.

Everything there needs me back:
the floods, the starving, the dark-souled.
To witness as the coffers
are covered with black velvet

and disappear.
To go behind the funeral procession
and wail. So many gone.

"Return, return!" plead the tiny
voices. "You'll have a place of honor
at the wakes; you'll have sweet foods."
But they don't even touch the silk robes
of belonging. This blood of longing.

The land's heartbreaking grasp,
its smother.
The dead keep quiet, but the soil
that barely covers them calls out.

But I am saved, I say.
And I am far.

At night the voices burrow
in my dreams and pluck
my broken heart strings.
They play dirges for the dead.
They cry all night.

IMMIGRANTS

for my parents

In our small hot kitchen
my parents cooked cho-cho
and callaloo, breadfruit

and the beautiful conch,
the lambi my father loved,
stewing it for hours

at a time, some part
of his island coming back
for him, his tongue.

Coconut milk, coconut water,
cloves and allspice,
ginger, curry, nutmeg –

all made that house
aromatic, made them forget
the mortgage of America,

the yoke of bills, companies.
Oh the taste of dasheen,
of saffron and mace,

all the spices of Jamaica
and Grenada transplanted
here, just as my parents

were transplanted, their
accents strange in this
nation that did not treasure

what they did: pigeon peas
and plantains, saltfish
and sugarcane, the sweet

sweet flesh of the tender
mango– yellow pulp easy
on the tongue, gracious

in the mouth, welcome
as any island song,
any calypso remembered

by daughters turned too American,
sons who know nothing of cassava
or guava, as any memory of home.

IN MY COUNTRY

walking by the waters
down where an honest river
shakes hands with the sea,
a woman passed round me
in a slow watchful circle,
as if I were a superstition;

or the worst dregs of her imagination,
so when she finally spoke
her words spliced into bars
of an old wheel. A segment of air.
Where do you come from?
"Here," I said, "Here. These parts."

JACKIE KAY (1961–)

PSALM FOR KINGSTON

If I forget thee, O Jerusalem
– Psalm 137

City of Jack Mandora – *mi nuh choose none* – of Anancy
prevailing over Mongoose, Breda Rat, Puss, and Dog, Anancy
saved by his wits in the midst of chaos and against all odds,
of bawdy Big Boy stories told by peacock-strutting boys, *hush-hush*
but loud enough to be heard by anyone passing by the yard.

City of market women at Half-Way-Tree with baskets
atop their heads or planted in front of their laps, squatting or standing
with arms akimbo, *susuing* with one another, clucking
their tongues, calling in voices of pure sugar, *Come dou-dou: see*
the pretty bag I have for you, then kissing their teeth when you saunter off.

City of school children in uniforms playing dandy
shandy
and brown girl in the ring – *tra-la-la-la-la* –
eating bun and cheese and bulla and mangoes,
juice sticky and running down their chins, bodies
arced
in laughter, mouths agape, heads thrown back.

City of old men with rheumy eyes, crouched in
doorways,
on verandahs, paring knives in hand, carving wood
pipes
or peeling sugar cane, of younger men pushing
carts
of roasted peanuts and oranges, calling out as they
walk the streets
and night draws near, of coconut vendors with
machetes in hand.

City where power cuts left everyone in sudden dark,
where the kerosene lamp's blue flame wavered on
kitchen walls,
where empty bellies could not be filled,
where *no eggs, no milk, no beef today* echoed
in shantytowns, around corners, down alleyways.

City where Marley sang, *Jah would never give the power to a baldhead*
while the baldheads reigned, where my parents chanted
down Babylon – *Fire! Burn! Jah! Rastafari! Selassie I!* –
where they paid weekly dues, saving for our passages back to Africa,
while in their beds my grandparents slept fitfully, dreaming of America.

City that lives under a long-memoried sun,
where the gunmen of my childhood are today's dons ruling neighbourhoods as fiefdoms, where violence
and beauty still lie down together. City of my birth –
if I forget thee, who will I be, singing the Lord's song in this strange land?

BROKEN MIRROR

I wake up to the speaking mirror.
To the tragedy, the scare
of the hitting bullet.
*
I cannot dare to look
at the mirror, looking
at the mirror looking back.
*
The bullet flew towards my head.
I ducked down and ran.
The bullet smashes the mirror,
shards scatter over the floor.
(Breathe –)
*
Today, I see the mirror
in the taxi window,
in the barber's shop.

BELARUSIAN 1

even our mothers have no idea how we were born
how we parted their legs and crawled out into the
world
the way you crawl from the ruins after a bombing
we couldn't tell which of us was a girl or a boy
we gorged on dirt thinking it was bread
and our future
a gymnast on a thin thread of the horizon
was performing there
at the highest pitch
bitch

we grew up in a country where
first your door is stroked with chalk
then at dark a chariot arrives
and no one sees you anymore
but riding in those cars were neither
armed men nor
a wanderer with a scythe
this is how love loved to visit us
and snatch us veiled

completely free only in public toilets
where for a little change nobody cared what we were
doing

we fought the summer heat the winter snow
when we discovered we ourselves were the language
and our tongues were removed we started talking
    with our eyes
when our eyes were poked out we talked with our hands
when our hands were cut off we conversed with our toes
when we were shot in the legs we nodded our heads
    for yes
and shook our heads for no and when they ate our
    heads alive
we crawled back into the bellies of our sleeping mothers
as if into bomb shelters
to be born again

and there on the horizon the gymnast of our future
was leaping through the fiery hoop
of the sun

THE PLACE IS LIT WITH MEMORY

1
Dejection is
to visit the ruins of your house in a dream
and return without having its dust clung to your
    hands.

2
Tenderness is
to water the withering flowers
in the neighbours' garden
because the flowers in your house dried up under
    bombardment.

3
Distance is
a geography of coercion.
– Thousands of miles separating two cities.
You left your clothes on the clothesline in the first
and in the second you extend your hands in the air
to collect your clothes from the balcony in the first.

4
Who can tell
your hand which is kept on the bell of your old house,
"Houses are not for those who left them"?

5
Only water
knows why flowers cry
in the balconies of happy homes
which we forsook.

6
On the way to your new house
there is a long avenue of nostalgia
in which you will walk forever.

7
When you touch the cold iron of the bus here,
a narcissus will grow on the iron handle of your
    house's door there:
This is how houses are faithful to their displaced
    owners.

8
You wake up every night in the middle of your sleep.
Water is still dripping from the tap in the sink of your
    old kitchen.

9
Life would not be so bad.
It will give you a new house.
But your soul will remain a wolf

that howls every night
on the stairs of your old house.

10
Your picture is watching the rain dropping
out the old window.
No one notices
that the wet beech tree is crying.

11
Darkness
grows in abandoned houses
like April's grass,
although the place is lit with memory.

TRANSLATED BY ALI ZNAIDI

RUTHENIA

I forget Ruthenia daily, fondly,
daisy chain of mountain hamlets
my ancestors fled – by foot, by rail,
by sail – forswearing Ruthenia: a cloud
of memories drifting from the simmering
peasant pot, or the Cold War

map I hunched above in grammar school.
For 500 years we barely evolved
in stateless Ruthenia, where religion
was the cabbage & the songbird
was the gypsy & the heraldic achievement
was the red bear on hind legs,

its tongue flicking, a field of silver
on the sinister side, stripes on the dexter,
split by the golden trident of Vladimir
the Great, which sounds baronial
but is true, as *The Primary Chronicle* records,
he chose Byzantium over Mecca –

after deliberation with boyars – because
Drinking is the joy of the Rus!
When I return to thee, Ruthenia, I will fly
by way of London, with vodka miniatures

& in-flight movies. I will kiss the earth,
I will peck each cheek – you never unlearn

Ruthenia (& its obsolete ethnonyms)
when your blood is from Ruthenia.
Like playing drinking games. I will forget
America slowly during my sojourn
among the oaks, the lindens, the Carpathian
ash, as I loaf in the undergrowth

& in the mezereum, in the honeysuckle
where I spy voles & black storks & the hazel
grouse, as I sigh aloud. But my mother is
America. I love to live in America where
the state religion is exuberance unregulated
& the songbird is the iPod

& the national pastime is ritualized violence.
It is 5,000 miles & seven centuries from *Rusynsko*
to New York & her beacon hand ablaze.
The land is light & harbor dark & the door
is always open, Ruthenia.
You alone are real to us.

GUYANA: SO NICE

for Savitri

Her visit home was so nice, except
the tenant had chopped down her fruit trees

and flowering trees and coconut
trees, to make a car lot for his failing

car sales business – you know those trees
back home you can pay somebody

to climb them and bring coconuts
right into your hands with their sweet milk

no he never asked her permission
but she felt so sorry for him you know

when he sold a car two men followed him
took his money, beat him up

threw him in their car trunk then left him
for dead in a ditch, but rain woke him

he crawled to the road and a taxi
took him to the hospital

never the same after that the poor man
returned to life but never well

he knows the names of the criminals
the whole neighborhood knows of course

the criminals pay the police this is why
so much crime occurs everyone is afraid

but seeing family back home, yes,
it is nice to visit back home sometimes.

DEAR REGIME,

After you've ground him into powder,
you can burn this to a fine ash. His family feels
it would be better off with nothing.

My father returned from Iran with everything but
his bones.
He said customs claimed them as government
property.
We laid him on a Persian carpet in front of the
television.
When I'd hold his wrist to his face
because he wanted to know the time,
we could see the holes made by swords in his elbow.
His arm reminded me of *kebab kubideh.*
It was hard for him to look outside;
he said the cumulus clouds
were too much like marrow
and he couldn't stand watching the dog
sniff the backyard, searching
for the rest of him. My sister and I put him to bed
thinking that beside our mother
he'd turn into himself,
but through the door we only heard him crying,
telling his wife he could never again make love,

and through the keyhole we saw her shivering
    with him
wrapped around her like an old blanket
until he died one morning.
She folded him into a rectangle,
mailing him in a white shoebox
back to his country.

WORKSHOP

The pale sound of jilgueros trilling in the jungle.
Abuelo rocks in his chair and maps the birds
in his head, practiced in the geometry of sound.

My uncle stokes the cabin's ironblack stove
with a short rod. The flames that come are his
loves. I cook – chile panameño, coconut milk –

a recipe I'd wanted to try. Abuelo eats,
suppresses the color that builds in his cheek.
To him the chile is a flash of snake in the mud.

He asks for plain rice, beans. Tío hugs his father,
kneels in front of the fire, whispers away the dying
of his little flames. We soak rice until

the water clouds. On the television, a fiesta . . .

The person I am showing the poem to
stops reading. He questions the TV,
circles it with a felt pen. "This feels so

out of place in a jungle to me. Can you
explain to the reader why it's there?"
For a moment, I can't believe.

You don't think we have 1930s technology?
The poem was trying to talk about stereotype,
gentleness instead of violence for once.

But now I should fill the little room
of my sonnet explaining how we own a TV?
A shame, because I had a great last line –

there was a parade in it, and a dancing
horse like you wouldn't believe.

MANGOES AT KROGER

What is this bullshit, I marvel
at the greenish, red-spotted kidney-like
mangoes that fit in my palms.
They're not like the ones from
my grandmother's tree –
those were as long as my forearm,
their skins yellow like the flesh
waiting beneath.

Each day, my grandfather's one chore
was to patiently sweep up the blanket
of leaves that covered the street.
My grandmother duct-taped
two broom handles together
to reach the taller branches
heavy with golden fruit.
A cloth sack tied to one end
of the stick sheathed gilt,
and we'd feast with our teeth
scraping the hard white pit,
tiny fibers wedged into gumline.

Passersby would tug at the low mangoes,
and my grandparents shrugged,
happy to share their wealth.

I can hear The Eagles on hidden speakers
while I hold a puny imported mango
and imagine the growers in Ecuador
keeping the best for themselves,
because what are the chances that
buyers here are missing a latitude
where this fruit hangs free for the taking,
a brown trickle of sticky amber
from the point where it was attached?

THE DANCING

In all these rotten shops, in all this broken furniture
and wrinkled ties and baseball trophies and
    coffee pots
I have never seen a post-war Philco
with the automatic eye
nor heard Ravel's "Bolero" the way I did
in 1945 in that tiny living room
on Beechwood Boulevard, nor danced as I did
then, my knives all flashing, my hair all streaming,
my mother red with laughter, my father cupping
his left hand under his armpit, doing the dance
of old Ukraine, the sound of his skin half drum,
half fart, the world at last a meadow,
the three of us whirling and singing, the three of us
screaming and falling, as if we were dying,
as if we could never stop – in 1945 –
in Pittsburgh, beautiful filthy Pittsburgh, home
of the evil Mellons, 5,000 miles away
from the other dancing – in Poland and Germany –
oh God of mercy, oh wild God.

GERALD STERN (1925–)

LAUREL

I'm sitting alone in my room

my clothes scattered around me,

and the suitcase that took to the road with me when
I fled

I keep telling it about our return, soon

When we go back, you'll carry my clothes that
crossed the border inside you

We'll pass through the cities, walk on their streets
once more

We'll write in the dust with our own ink

and our ink to us will be attar and laurel

 FADWA SULEIMAN (1970–2017)
TRANSLATED BY MARILYN HACKER

SEA GRAPES

That sail which leans on light,
tired of islands,
a schooner beating up the Caribbean

for home, could be Odysseus,
home-bound on the Aegean;
that father and husband's

longing, under gnarled sour grapes, is
like the adulterer hearing Nausicaa's name
in every gull's outcry.

This brings nobody peace. The ancient war
between obsession and responsibility
will never finish and has been the same

for the sea-wanderer or the one on shore
now wriggling on his sandals to walk home,
since Troy sighed its last flame,

and the blind giant's boulder heaved the trough
from whose groundswell the great hexameters come
to the conclusions of exhausted surf.

The classics can console. But not enough.

DEREK WALCOTT (1930–2017)

4th MOVEMENT

We collect languages, flags, learn
to cook macaroni and cheese, drink coffee,
and replace Googoosh with Madonna,
Gharib Afshar with Jay Leno,
but make no mistake, we never lose

our voice. *Seda, Seda,* said Forugh Farrokhzad,
tanha sedast. Seda keh jazbeh
zare-hayeh jahan khahad shod.
Chera Tavaghof konam?

I channel her voice:

Voice, voice, only voice remains.
Voice seeping into time.
Why should I stop?

LABOR

THE MECHANIC

Stretching over the carburetor,
he shouts about the quality of life here
compared to back home, how they stood
in line for bread, how there were no cedars
more green than those by the shore.

He could be my uncle in Syria, 1948,
a man taking in fumes, a cigarette balancing
on a fender, hands lined with grease,
saving coins in a jar for his newborn,
losing relatives to malaria, to civil war.

But today we're in Hollywood – the palms
dry. This man speaks to me in Armenian.
He remembers working late into the Lebanese night,
the plaza's noise of backgammon boards,
headlights beaming beyond the Mediterranean.

Now, he's used to customers calling out
his American nickname, while he wrenches
spark plugs into place, the old country
preserved on a calendar. He's used to this
new world of dollar bills, available parts.

I say bless him and this hand-made auto shop,
the first opening, closing of hoods, pump of pistons.
And bless the one who never made it over
the Atlantic, an arm extending into the engine,
a scar exposed, the shape of an eagle's wing.

WHAT COULD THE TITLE POSSIBLY BE

He kissed his wife and kids
maybe he wished them a good
day in Spanish, maybe in some
form of North American
English, maybe some other way,
maybe he said *see you tonight,*
maybe stopped at the door
turned around: *I love you,*
got in the car, went to the first
of two jobs. He'd been working
at the restaurant for ten years.
He was "loved." He was
"diligent." A "model" "citizen."
Some good voters with money
in the bank wearing white
headlights I mean skin were
stunned this could happen so
close to home. So close to
the expensive food he served
them. The card, green as the
lawns, was in the mail. Some
authority said. Another said
that doesn't matter.
The sheriff at the local jail said
sure we'll keep him. The local

democrats said It's ok, it's only
ICE, meaning not US. The
weekly printed he had an old
dwi. When they took him
they forgot to tell him
anything. When they took him
across states and borders
with no access to counsel
they neglected to remember
he was a man with a family
and a place he now called home,
holding more than one job. They
did remember he was brown
spoke a language many didn't
understand, from a hot country
green as the missing card.
They did remember
it didn't matter. When they
took Luis they were just
doing their job.

TO THE BANGLADESHI CAB DRIVER IN SAN FRANCISCO

Half-drunk, I don't do more than lean
my head against the back of your seat,
straining to hear. You call your brother

to wake him from slumber. We drive up
hills past palm trees and sidewalks chalked
yellow, your voice soft as you murmur

in the language fed to me from birth.
I strain to hear each known word:
bhai=brother, bon=sister, bhaat=rice,

daal=lentils. After the nightly fares, do you
replace slacks for a lunghi, shoes for chappals?
Do you close your fingers into the sharp beak

of a hungry crow to gather the last bits
of bhaat and daal? I could open my mouth to you
in the register I know we know, but don't,

or won't. I can't go back to summers spent unfurling
in heat beside vendors uncapping bottles of Fanta, just
to weave hours striped with palm trees into jute-
joyous

shacks. Bhai, here it is spring. Drive past
these parks of dew-carcassed grass, the smooth
and bright limbs heaped carelessly. Drive

ocean-ward. Park at the dock, where used
condoms remain half-submerged in sand.
Cyan water will forgive bottles bullied

into shards, such glittering emerald ghosts
of revelry or remorse. Swim homeward. There,
it's noon: time enough for the sun to coax out

the perfume of a shapla lily's pink petals,
kissed by the lips of a garment worker
whose ankle sings with bells as she pedals.

HOW I AM

Once upon a time I knew how I was doing.
Now I find out from day to day how I am:
"Well, thank you, and you?"
Distantly related to all the black female cashiers,
to all the gymnasts from Chinatown,
to all the code numbers, card numbers, Pin and Pam
    numbers
I push a button again, I leave jokes on the answering
    machines,
touched by their soft voice which asks me to stay on
    hold a little longer
because my call is important to them,
I am the most important person in the world and
    I stay on hold
until I fall asleep with my hand on the buttons,
remembering how in childhood I played nurse
among the whispers of the women in the kitchen
who were boiling plum jam and telling stories about
    our sinful fathers,
those wonderful men who came home late with hot
    loaves of bread.

I am definitely the most important, buried under bills,
receipts,
life and death insurance policies and offers of
vacations on exotic islands
I listened to my heartbeats – Pin, Pin – in the howl of
the ambulances,
fire trucks, police cars, vehicles in which I would run
away
into the wide and good world and whatever I end up
doing:
"I am well. Nice to have met me."

 CARMEN FIRAN (1958–)
TRANSLATED BY ISAIAH SHEFFER
WITH THE POET

A FLUSHING VILLANELLE

Slightly Edited Lines from "The Case of Jane Doe Ponytail"
by Barry and Singer, New York Times

As she grew older, she caught and collected the
enchanting butterflies
zigzagging by the river, meticulously preserving their
fragile iridescence.
I want to go to work, the girl would say to her
parents. I want to pick ginseng.

Then she left for 40th Road, a gritty street of
commerce in Flushing
where strivers, dawdlers, and passers-by are oblivous
to what is transpiring.
I want to go to work, the girl had said to her parents.
I want to pick ginseng.

More than once in a massage parlor, a man beat her
about the face.
An officer, a gun held to her head, forced her to
perform oral sex.
Once she had caught and collected the enchanting
butterflies and

friends had marveled at her collection book, asking to keep one.
She was fond of Heineken, Red Bull and Colombian rotisserie chicken.
I want to go to work, the girl had said to her parents. I want to pick ginseng.

In the end, SiSi, given name Song Yang, fleeing a cop working vice,
leaped from her balcony, hit the pavement, died in the ambulance.
As a little girl, she'd caught and collected the enchanting butterflies.

Her competitors considered her territorial and tireless. A shop owner
said, "I hear she was No. 1: young, pretty, and great service."
She once caught and collected enchanting butterflies zigzagging by the river.
I want to pick ginseng, little Song Yang had said. She was a born worker.

BARGAIN

On his first weekend in America
I hired him as a watchman.
Though he was six
he wanted to make some money.

I told him, "There are twelve keys
at different places in this factory.
Every hour I go through them all.
See this clock? I carry it
and punch it at each place.
They pay me seven dollars an hour
and I'll give you three
if you make a round for me.

"It's a good bargain, isn't it?
When I served in the Chinese army
I made six yuan a month. How much
is that in American money? –
just a dollar.

"Now in one day you can make
more than I did in a year.
Don't be scared.
I will go with you."

He was happy
capering ahead with the clock
as we passed the quiet machines.

THE NIGHT WATCHMAN

In gratitude, every six years
The Homeland sends him a new
Prosthesis, thus returning him to
A corporal's wisdom, which is not at all
His own: he had wanted to be
A schoolmaster, a doctor,
Or a grandfather in a country
Of brown earth and of swallows
Weaving against the slightest backlight
A vast fabric of dreams.
At his window, he watches for the moment
When the streetlights go out
In the flat and airless night.
He knows the last cry will be his own.

HÉDI KADDOUR (1945–)
TRANSLATED BY MARILYN HACKER

ON THE BIRTH OF GOOD & EVIL DURING THE LONG WINTER OF '28

When the streetcar stalled on Joy Road,
the conductor finished his coffee, puffed
into his overcoat, and went to phone in.
The Hungarian punch press operator wakened
alone, 7000 miles from home, pulled down
his orange cap and set out. If he saw
the winter birds scuffling in the cinders,
if he felt this was the dawn of a new day,
he didn't let on. Where the sidewalks
were unshovelled, he stamped on, raising
his galoshes a little higher with each step.
I came as close as I dared and could hear
only the little gasps as the cold entered
the stained refectory of the breath.
I could see by the way the blue tears squeezed
from the dark of the eyes, by the way
his moustache first dampened and then froze,
that as he turned down Dexter Boulevard,
he considered the hosts of the dead,
and nearest among them, his mother-in-law,
who darkened his table for twenty-seven years
and bruised his wakings. He considered how
before she went off in the winter of '27
she had knitted this cap, knitted so slowly

that Christmas came and went, and now he could
forgive her at last for the twin wool lappets
that closed perfectly on a tiny metal snap
beneath the chin and for making all of it orange.

STARLIGHT HAVEN

Susie Wong was at the Starlight Haven,
the Good Times Bar and Sailors' Home.
It was always dark at noon –
you had to blink three times before
you could see Susie standing by
the washed chutney jar half filled
with ten- and twenty-cent coins.
When the bar was empty her eyes were sad,
and she'd mop the Formica tables,
dry a row of tall Anchor Pilsner
glasses. The wet cloth slapped-slapped
like Susie's Japanese slippers
over the dirty floor.
                    Then the swing doors
bang and the darkness is full of white
uniforms, full of cold Tigers
sweating in warm air-conditioning.

I think of the flutter in Susie's pulse –
Buy a drink, Tommy boy! G.I. Joe!
Yankee Doodle! Howdy Doody! Romeo! –
and suddenly Johnny Mathis
like black magic is crooning "Chances Are."
Her girlish voice is soft and happy,
soft like a tubby belly after

six babies and ten years of beat-up
marriage, happy as only Singapore
Susie Wongs can be, when Johnny
and Ray are rocking the bottles
and their tops pop off and the chutney
jar is singing chink, chink.
The red-faced brawny men are laughing
at her voice. Quack, quack, they laugh
so hard they spill Tigers over
the plastic counter. Quack, quack, fuck, fuck.
Susie looks at the bar-man who makes
his coolie eyes dumb black stones
and wipes up the yellow puddles
without a grunt.
Thirty years later
I hear mother singing "In the sweet
by and by." She is a Jesus woman
grown up from bar-girl. Sailors and Tommies
have disappeared from her Memory Lane.
I still keep the bracelet mother gave me,
gold saved from beer spilled on the clean
tables, her clean lap. I savor the taste
of that golden promise, never to love men
in white who laugh, quack, quack, fuck, fuck.

THE CONTRACT SAYS: WE'D LIKE THE CONVERSATION TO BE BILINGUAL

When you come, bring your brown-
ness so we can be sure to please

the funders. Will you check this
box; we're applying for a grant.

Do you have any poems that speak
to troubled teens? Bilingual is best.

Would you like to come to dinner
with the patrons and sip Patrón?

Will you tell us the stories that make
us uncomfortable, but not complicit?

Don't read us the one where you
are just like us. Born to a green house,

garden, don't tell us how you picked
tomatoes and ate them in the dirt

watching vultures pick apart another
bird's bones in the road. Tell us the one

about your father stealing hubcaps
after a colleague said that's what his

kind did. Tell us how he came
to the meeting wearing a poncho

and tried to sell the man his hubcaps
back. Don't mention your father

was a teacher, spoke English, loved
making beer, loved baseball, tell us

again about the poncho, the hubcaps,
how he stole them, how he did the thing

he was trying to prove he didn't do.

UNDERGROUND PEARLS

My great-grandfather sent by Austrians
To look for pearls underground,
In potato skins,
Overwhelmed by exhaustion and shame
Never came back

My grandfather would have picked them up
On his knees between the wars
One night before they were ripened
Twisting the weeds
Which scratched our history on the fences.
With Colorado bugs
He signed on a piece of burned land
A secret pact
Found later when too old
He was preaching in the village about globalization
And how to make potatoes round in general.

My father avoided them
In all urban cultures from the balcony
Where the classics agonized in cheap editions
Bloomed unexpectedly.

On the asphalt at the corner of my house
Lies a wound of stone
There three McDonalds went bankrupt
Haunted by the ghosts of the potatoes
Fried in vain.

MEXICANS BEGIN JOGGING

At the factory I worked
In the fleck of rubber, under the press
Of an oven yellow with flame,
Until the border patrol opened
Their vans and my boss waved for us to run.
"Over the fence, Soto," he shouted,
And I shouted that I was American.
"No time for lies," he said, and pressed
A dollar in my palm, hurrying me
Through the back door.

Since I was on his time, I ran
And became the wag to a short tail of Mexicans –
Ran past the amazed crowds that lined
The street and blurred like photographs, in rain.
I ran from that industrial road to the soft
Houses where people paled at the turn of an autumn
    sky.
What could I do but yell *vivas*
To baseball, milkshakes, and those sociologists
Who would clock me
As I jog into the next century
On the power of a great, silly grin.

PEACHES

A crate of peaches straight from the farm
has to be maintained, or eaten in days.
Obvious, but in my family, they went so fast,
I never saw the mess that punishes delay.

I thought everyone bought fruit by the crate,
stored it in the coolest part of the house,
then devoured it before any could rot.
I'm from the Peach State, and to those

who ask *But where are you from originally*,
I'd like to reply *The homeland of the peach*,
but I'm too nice, and they might not look it up.
In truth, the reason we bought so much

did have to do with being Chinese – at least
Chinese in that part of America, both strangers
and natives on a lonely, beautiful street
where food came in stackable containers

and fussy bags, unless you bothered to drive
to the source, where the same money landed
a bushel of fruit, a twenty-pound sack of rice.
You had to drive anyway, each house surrounded

by land enough to grow your own, if lawns
hadn't been required. At home I loved to stare
into the extra freezer, reviewing mountains
of foil-wrapped meats, cakes, juice concentrate,

mysterious packets brought by house guests
from New York Chinatown, to be transformed
by heat, force, and my mother's patient effort,
enough to keep us fed through flood or storm,

provided the power stayed on, or fire and ice
could be procured, which would be labor-intensive,
but so was everything else my parents did.
Their lives were labor, they kept this from the kids,

who grew up to confuse work with pleasure,
to become typical immigrants' children,
taller than their parents and unaware of hunger
except when asked the odd, perplexing question.

LANGUAGE

DO YOU SPEAK PERSIAN?

Some days we can see Venus in midafternoon. Then at
night, stars
separated by billions of miles, light traveling years

to die in the back of an eye.

Is there a vocabulary for this – one to make dailiness
amplify
and not diminish wonder?

I have been so careless with the words I already have.

I don't remember how to say *home*
in my first language, or *lonely*, or *light*.

I remember only
delam barat tang shodeh, I miss you,

and *shab bekheir*, good night.

How is school going, Kaveh-joon?
Delam barat tang shodeh.

Are you still drinking?
Shab bekheir.

For so long every step I've taken
has been from one tongue to another.

To order the world:
I need, you need, he/she/it needs.

The rest, left to a hungry jackal
in the back of my brain.

Right now our moon looks like a pale cabbage rose.
Delam barat tang shodeh.

We are forever folding into the night.
Shab bekheir.

BROKE

While I study my aunt makes a few bucks with no English at the Au Bon Pain in Harvard Square. She's sweeping like it's a Saturday morning in her Cape Verdean home. Don't stop until the floor's licked clean. Make your bed like you changed your bed. Today my aunt introduces her *subrinha* to the other Cape Verdean workers, who, young and old, are mostly cleaning or organizing the croissants. I smile over, a free Americano. It takes courage or will or common sense or common courtesy or respect to dare a language not your own. When they ask me how I'm doing in broken English, I hurry toward class but today my aunt has my grandmother on her phone. *Pamódi, pamódi,* Vovo wants to know why I don't visit. She's yelling at me in Kriolu and I love how it sounds to be loved so fiercely in another language. I hear words I know and ones I don't in the voice of the only woman who braided my hair, the only woman who held my hand in her baby-soft skin. I want to ask Vovo how she's doing, but she doesn't know any English. Across the room, one woman mistakenly teaches another to say, I miss you, have a good day.

ENGLISH FLAVORS

I love to lick English the way I licked the hard
round licorice sticks the Belgian nuns gave me for six
good conduct points on Sundays after mass.

Love it when "plethora," "indolence," "damask,"
or my new word: "lasciviousness," stain my tongue,
thicken my saliva, sweet as those sticks – black

and slick with every lick it took to make daggers
out of them: sticky spikes I brandished straight up
to the ebony crucifix in the dorm, with the pride

of a child more often punished than praised.
"Amuck," "awkward," or "knuckles," have jaw-
breaker flavors; there's honey in "hunter's moon,"

hot pepper in "hunk," and "mellifluous" has aromas
of almonds and milk. Those tastes of recompense
still bittersweet today as I roll, bend and shape

English in my mouth, repeating its syllables
like acts of contrition, then sticking out my new
tongue –
flavored and sharp – to the ambiguities of meaning.

IGUANA

for A. T.

My friend from Guyana
was asked in Philadelphia
if she was from "Iguana."

Iguana, which crawls and then
stills, which flicks its tongue at the sun.

In history we learned that Lucayans
ate iguana, that Caribs
(my grandmother's people)
ate Lucayans (the people of Guanahani).
Guiana (the colonial way,
with an i, southern-most
of the Caribbean) is iguana; Inagua
(southern-most of The Bahamas,
northern-most of the Caribbean)
is iguana. Inagua, crossroads with Haiti,
Inagua of the salt and flamingos.
The Spanish called it *Heneagua*,
"water is to be found there,"
water, water everywhere.

Guyana (in the language of Arawaks,
Wai Ana, "Land of Many Waters")

is iguana, veins running through land,
grooves between green scales.
My grandmother from Moruga,
(southern-most in Trinidad)
knew the names of things.
She rubbed iguana with bird pepper,
she cooked its sweet meat.

The earth is on the back
of an ageless iguana.

We are all from the Land of Iguana,
Hewanorra, Carib name for St. Lucia.

And all the iguanas scurry away from me.
And all the iguanas are dying.

RULES FOR A CHINESE CHILD BUYING STATIONERY IN A LONDON BOOKSHOP

Speak to the white
elderly man at the counter.
There will be many

more of them
in your life, but start
with him. Recall those syllables

you've whispered over and
over like some version
of the Lord's Prayer:

Our Father who art
in heaven and is
white and beyond skin.

Enunciate. He must hear
what you have to say
if you are to be helped.

Begin with *please.* Say
may I. End with *thank you.*
He will be delighted

to know you are polite,
soft-spoken, well-mannered.
You will be overjoyed

at his acceptance, a palm
reaching towards you
for something you are able to give.

You must hand over the money
quickly, but not in haste.
Your parents' wisdom comes

from *having had more salt*
than you have eaten rice.
This proverb is untranslatable,

but memorise and trust
in it all the same.
You are a tiny machine

being oiled
for the day you must
face the world,

a lifetime ahead of you,
years of salt
and rice and tea.

AH, ACH, VAI BILINGVISM

From what language do you begin to drive your
    sentence?
In what direction?
Which way do you translate?
From your native tongue to your childhood
or from the new to think yourself into the world
that is your home now?

In what language do you dream?
I don't dream in language. I dream in pictures.
Sometimes people from long ago
who spoke in my old language
appear in my dreams. Are they from there
or from here where I dream them?
In my dreams I sometimes read in a language
I never spoke or read but I'm dream-fluent in.
No one speaks in any language in my dreams
yet there it is, written and spoken by someone
I forgot already when I wake up.
I have no idea what that gibberish is on the tape.
You shouldn'ta done all that dreaming, girl.
Does here start there or here?
Is it arabic or sanskrit and is there still
a calendar on the wall gregorian or hebrew
that isn't about time   a calendar of stories.

The place you are what once you were is there
lost in one of those nonsense tales
that was somehow both home and elsewhere.
And where are they now who knew you there?
When you travel between languages what suit
do you wear, what suitcase do you carry?

GUERILLAGARDENWRITINGPOEM

The mouth of the city is tongued with tar
its glands gutter saliva, teeth chatter in rail
clatter, throat echoes car horns and tyre's
screech, forging new language: a brick city
smoke-speak of stainless steel consonants
and suffocated vowels. These are trees and
shrubbery, the clustered flora battling all
hours, staccato staggered through streets.

Meet Rich and Eleanor on Brabourn Grove
as he wrestles her wheelbarrow over cobble-
stones to the traffic island by Kitto Road
where this night, coloured a turquoise-grit,
cathedral-quiet and saintly, makes prayer
of their whispers and ritual of their work:
bend over, clear rubble, cut weed and plant.

But more than seeds are sown here. You
can tell by his tender pat on tended patch;
the soft cuff to a boy's head – first day to
school, by how they rest with parent-pride
against stone walls, huff into winter's cold,
press faces together as though tulips might
stem from two lips, gather spades, forks,
weeds and go. Rich wheelbarrows back to

Eleanor's as vowels flower or flowers vowel
through smoke-speak, soil softens, the city
drenched with new language thrills and
the drains are drunk with dreams.

The sky sways on the safe side of tipsy
and it's altogether an alien time of half-
life and hope, an after-fight of gentle fog
and city smog, where the debris of dew drips

to this narrative of progress, this city tale;
this story is my story, this vista my song.
I cluster in the quiet, stack against steel
seek islands, hope, and a pen to sow with.

BILINGUAL/BILINGÜE

My father liked them separate, one there,
one here (allá y aquí), as if aware

that words might cut in two his daughter's heart
(el corazón) and lock the alien part

to what he was – his memory, his name
(su nombre) – with a key he could not claim.

"English outside this door, Spanish inside,"
he said, "y basta." But who can divide

the world, the word (mundo y palabra) from
any child? I knew how to be dumb

and stubborn (testaruda); late, in bed,
I hoarded secret syllables I read

until my tongue (mi lengua) learned to run
where his stumbled. And still the heart was one.

I like to think he knew that, even when,
proud (orgulloso) of his daughter's pen,

he stood outside mis versos, half in fear
of words he loved but wanted not to hear.

RHINA P. ESPAILLAT (1932–)

LAND

The noble man does not alight upon an easy land,
and flight will not avail the lowly.
– al-Hārīth b. Ḥilliza

1.
These words,
I saw them quickly cross the field
and the space awakened.
Words,
when they pass the frail trees,
the trees become heavy with tears.
Words,
they are the lost homeland
and we, the rubble and remains.

2.
Homeland
has become desolate with us.
We set out before light
but found no way.
Homeland,
we speak it and we name it,
and the words and names weep.
Homeland
spins in a limp age

deafened by echoes.
How did time become so small?
Its yellow shadows despise us.
There's nothing but astonishment
in every direction,
and if you walk, the roads deceive.

3.
Words,
we live in,
when there's nowhere to settle
and the directions themselves close down.
Words,
they are home,
the land and the sky to us
and everything between.

JAWDAT FAKHREDDINE (1953–)
TRANSLATED BY HUDA FAKHREDDINE
AND JAYSON IWEN

SHOYN FERGÉSSIN: "I'VE FORGOTTEN" IN YIDDISH

But now it's the Yiddish itself I'm forgetting;
it's back on the wharf, in a grimed-over jar
we can barely see into. What's this: is it a cameo
brooch,
the bride's profile eaten-at by pickle-brine; or
is it a slice of radish? This is a tooth,
yes? We can turn that jar in the sun all day and
not be able to read it. There's a label, with a name
in black script dancing just beyond arm's reach.

A woman is weeping. What did he *do*? he asks
the noncommittal stars, the dark and rhythmic water,
even the slimy pilings. This is a wharf,
in summer. He tells her a joke, not that
it does much good. This is my grandfather,
Louie (in English). This is my grandmother, *Rosie.*
1912. They're in each other's arms again by morning
and don't need to say a word.

We'll find them, like ancient coins or arrowheads.
Now they can only be approximate. Here, washed up
on the beach: a few maxims, song titles, even that joke.
It goes: " 'You're a Jew, how come you have a name
like Sean Ferguson?' He says, 'I was so frightened
when we landed at Ellis Island that I couldn't remember
anything for a minute. So that's what I said. They
    asked me
my name and I said *I've forgotten.'* "

ASSIMILATION

It was only a matter of time
I raised my voice from the second story
and did not respond, *Perdón?*

I had down the Valley girl *like,*
hugged my binder and books
close to my chest, like in *Clueless,*

all of my weight on one leg
so the other could be all
like this. First, *What?* then *What-*

ever, the disrespectful American
words stinking up his house,
my held breath as I waited for him

to set the pestle down,
the cutting board, the stalks, the cleaver –
everything in his hands out of his hands.

ELEGY FOR JOSEPH BRODSKY

In plain speech, for the sweetness
between the lines is no longer important,
what you call immigration I call suicide.
I am sending, behind the punctuation,
unfurling nights of New York, avenues
slipping into Cyrillic –
winter coils words, throws snow on a wind.
You, in the middle of an unwritten sentence, stop,
exile to a place further than silence.

I left your Russia for good, poems sewn into my pillow
rushing towards my own training
to live with your lines
on a verge of a story set against itself.
To live with your lines, those where sails rise, waves
beat against the city's granite in each vowel, –
pages open by themselves, a quiet voice
speaks of suffering, of water.

We come back to where we have committed a crime,
we don't come back to where we loved, you said;
your poems are wolves nourishing us with their milk.
I tried to imitate you for two years. It feels like burning

and singing about burning. I stand
as if someone spat at me.
You would be ashamed of these wooden lines,
how I don't imagine your death
but it is here, setting my hands on fire.

PERSIMMONS

In sixth grade Mrs. Walker
slapped the back of my head
and made me stand in the corner
for not knowing the difference
between *persimmon* and *precision.*
How to choose

persimmons. This is precision.
Ripe ones are soft and brown-spotted.
Sniff the bottoms. The sweet one
will be fragrant. How to eat:
put the knife away, lay down newspaper.
Peel the skin tenderly, not to tear the meat.
Chew the skin, suck it,
and swallow. Now, eat
the meat of the fruit,
so sweet,
all of it, to the heart.

Donna undresses, her stomach is white.
In the yard, dewy and shivering
with crickets, we lie naked,
face-up, face-down.
I teach her Chinese.
Crickets: *chiu chiu.* Dew: I've forgotten.

Naked: I've forgotten.
Ni, wo: you and me.
I part her legs,
remember to tell her
she is beautiful as the moon.

Other words
that got me into trouble were
fight and *fright*, *wren* and *yarn*.
Fight was what I did when I was frightened,
fright was what I felt when I was fighting.
Wrens are small, plain birds,
yarn is what one knits with.
Wrens are soft as yarn.
My mother made birds out of yarn.
I loved to watch her tie the stuff;
a bird, a rabbit, a wee man.

Mrs. Walker brought a persimmon to class
and cut it up
so everyone could taste
a *Chinese apple.* Knowing
it wasn't ripe or sweet, I didn't eat
but watched the other faces.

My mother said every persimmon has a sun
inside, something golden, glowing,
warm as my face.

Once, in the cellar, I found two wrapped in newspaper,
forgotten and not yet ripe.
I took them and set both on my bedroom windowsill,
where each morning a cardinal
sang, *The sun, the sun.*

Finally understanding
he was going blind,
my father sat up all one night
waiting for a song, a ghost.
I gave him the persimmons,
swelled, heavy as sadness,
and sweet as love.

This year, in the muddy lighting
of my parents' cellar, I rummage, looking
for something I lost.
My father sits on the tired, wooden stairs,
black cane between his knees,
hand over hand, gripping the handle.
He's so happy that I've come home.
I ask how his eyes are, a stupid question.
All gone, he answers.

Under some blankets, I find a box.
Inside the box I find three scrolls.
I sit beside him and untie
three paintings by my father:
Hibiscus leaf and a white flower.
Two cats preening.
Two persimmons, so full they want to drop from
    the cloth.

He raises both hands to touch the cloth,
asks, *Which is this?*

This is persimmons, Father.

Oh, the feel of the wolftail on the silk,
the strength, the tense
precision in the wrist.
I painted them hundreds of times
eyes closed. These I painted blind.
Some things never leave a person:
scent of the hair of one you love,
the texture of persimmons,
in your palm, the ripe weight.

ILLEGAL IMMIGRATION

Is the absence of a paper
and the presence of a person.

A person with pages
and pages documenting

her movements is a convict.
Or undocumented.

Who is made to say, *My name is.*
Who is made to say, *I am the child of.*

Immigration wants to know the names
of your parents. The names of their parents.

A people with lineage can still be scattered.
Is the son of Abraham. Is the son of Isaac. Is the son
of Jacob.

People who do not know about documents
do not need them.

They have never needed them.
A person with documents

is the one who must bear them aloft.
They will set her hand on fire.

It takes place in the bathroom
of a border patrol station.

Kingsville, Texas.
All at once, she needs to drink, piss, crap.

Her period comes. The agent says,
No you can't go to your mother.

Illegal immigration began with a law.
It ends with a new law.

She may not step onto a cattle car.
She may die on foot. In the fields.

In labor. In custody.
You know what is happening.

She speaks. She is speaking.
My name is. I am the child of.

See if that works.

LORD, SPANGLISH ME

i.
Lord, Spanglish mi abuela para mi

boil the orange rind
beneath the syntax
peeled of her name

translate *naranja* into *familia*
the grove into tea,
the tea into the talisman

of her hand's soft work,
the color of fold,

unfolded,
& sung.

ii.
Lord, Spanglish mi abuela para mi

her kingdom creation come,
her gray hair grown down the fears,

her pale hand plucking
my tears as plums

as love ransoms

the noun within,
her childhood unseeded

        beneath the ravage,
the creek drowning

her colony home,
the aphids   & the oak,

her velvet Christ flood-spent,
            & Godless.

iii.
Lord, Spanglish mi madre para ti

carve shipless the light
my world is etched by
the wreck-salt
so she may move
among the beryl water,
tide red with the silt
beneath baptism, her eyes cast
in the shadow of the soft
of lavender grown there.

iv.
Lord, Spanglish mi lengua para ti

    that I may break open
    the promise-space of my fear,
    & become ladder, &

I may finally skin my ravage,

    that I may bear the estranged seasons,
    for I know we are creatures of metal
    without answer,

    a lost Spring
    whose lips rest
    where intimacy resigned
            the shapes of want,

    our honey succored from dust.

MY FAITHFUL MOTHER TONGUE

Faithful mother tongue,
I have been serving you.
Every night, I used to set before you little bowls of
 colors
so you could have your birch, your cricket, your finch
as preserved in my memory.

This lasted many years.
You were my native land; I lacked any other.
I believed that you would also be a messenger
between me and some good people
even if they were few, twenty, ten
or not born, as yet.

Now, I confess my doubt.
There are moments when it seems to me I have
 squandered my life.
For you are a tongue of the debased,
of the unreasonable, hating themselves
even more than they hate other nations,
a tongue of informers,
a tongue of the confused,
ill with their own innocence.

But without you, who am I?
Only a scholar in a distant country,
a success, without fears and humiliations.
Yes, who am I without you?
Just a philosopher, like everyone else.

I understand, this is meant as my education:
the glory of individuality is taken away,
Fortune spreads a red carpet
before the sinner in a morality play
while on the linen backdrop a magic lantern throws
images of human and divine torture.

Faithful mother tongue,
perhaps after all it's I who must try to save you.
So I will continue to set before you little bowls
 of colors
bright and pure if possible,
for what is needed in misfortune is a little order
 and beauty.

Berkeley, 1968

ARABIC
(Jordan, 1992)

The man with laughing eyes stopped smiling
to say, "Until you speak Arabic –
– you will not understand pain."

Something to do with the back of the head,
an Arab carries sorrow in the back of the head
that only language cracks, the thrum of stones

weeping, grating hinge on an old metal gate.
"Once you know," he whispered, "you can enter the
room
whenever you need to. Music you heard from a
distance,

the slapped drum of a stranger's wedding,
wells up inside your skin, inside rain, a thousand
pulsing tongues. You are changed."

Outside, the snow had finally stopped.
In a land where snow rarely falls,
we had felt our days grow white and still.

I thought pain had no tongue. Or every tongue
at once, supreme translator, sieve. I admit my
shame. To live on the brink of Arabic, tugging

its rich threads without understanding
how to weave the rug . . . I have no gift.
The sound, but not the sense.

I kept looking over his shoulder for someone else
to talk to, recalling my dying friend who only scrawled
I can't write. What good would any grammar have been

to her then? I touched his arm, held it hard,
which sometimes you don't do in the Middle East, and
said,
I'll work on it, feeling sad

for his good strict heart, but later in the slick street
hailed a taxi by shouting *Pain!* and it stopped
in every language and opened its doors.

WHERE I AM NOT

I ask the new migrant if he regrets leaving Russia.
We have dispensed already with my ancestry.
He says no. For a time, he was depressed. He found
with every return he missed what he left behind.
A constant state of this. Better to love by far
where you are. He taps the steering wheel of his car,
the hum of the engine an imperceptible tremble
in us. When he isn't driving, he works tending
to new trees. I've seen these saplings popping
up all over the suburbs, tickling the bellies
of bridges, the new rooted darlings of the State.
The council spent a quarter mil on them &
someone, he – Lilian – must ensure the dirt
holds. Gentrification is climate-friendly now.
I laugh and he laughs, and we eat the distance
between histories. He checks on his buds daily.
Are they okay? They are okay. They do not need
him, but he speaks, and they listen or at least
shake a leaf. What a world where you can live off
land by loving it. If only we cared for each other
this way. The council cares for their investment.
The late greenery, that is, not Lilian, who shares
his ride on the side. I wonder what it would cost
to have men be tender to me regularly,
to be folded into his burly, to be left on the side

of the road as he drove away, exhausted. Even
my dreams of tenderness involve being used
& I'm not sure who to blame: colonialism,
capitalism, patriarchy, queerness or poetry?
Sorry, this is a commercial for the Kia Sportage
now. This is a commercial for Lilian's thighs.
He didn't ask for this and neither did I – how
language drapes us together, how stories tongue
each other in the back seat and the sky blurs
out of frame. There are too many agonies
to discuss here, and I am nearly returned.
He has taken me all the way back, around
the future flowering, back to where I am not,
to the homes I keep investing in as harms.
I should fill them with trees. Let the boughs
cover the remembered boy, cowering
under a mother, her raised weapon
not the cane but the shattering within,
let the green tear through the wall
paper, let life replace memory. Lilian, I left
you that day, and in the leaving, a love
followed. Isn't that a wonder and a wound?
Tell me which it is, I confess I mistake the two.
I walk up the stairs to my old brick apartment
where the peach tree reaches for the railing,
a few blushing fruits poking through the bars,
eager to brush my leg, to say linger, halt.

I want to stop, to hold it for real, just once
but I must wait until I am safe.

THE GIFT

a b c   a b c   a b c

She doesn't know what comes after.
So we begin again:

a b c   a b c   a b c

But I can see the fourth letter:
a strand of black hair – unraveled
from the alphabet
& written
on her cheek.

Even now the nail salon
will not leave her: isopropyl acetate,
ethyl acetate, chloride, sodium lauryl
sulfate & sweat fuming
through her pink
I ❤ NY t-shirt.

a b c   a b c   a – the pencil snaps.

The *b* bursting its belly
as dark dust blows
through a blue-lined sky.

Don't move, she says, as she picks
a wing bone of graphite
from the yellow carcass, slides it back
between my fingers.
Again. & again

I see it: the strand of hair lifting
from her face . . . how it fell
onto the page – & lived
with no sound. Like a word.
I still hear it.

BORN IN HUNGARIAN

Your stone says *Born In Hungarian*
a country foreign to local stone cutters
unlike Gallatin Madison Murfreesboro

a strange place to have come from
whose streets mapped out a language
in your head a message saying nowhere

no one speaks your language any more
not the dead who followed you to
Nashville setting up their small

orthodox temple nor the living
who visit only on occasion driving
through a ghetto a word

you fled from to get here wherever
your descendants go they are at home
strange only to themselves other

silent countries surround you Polish
Russian Lithuanian my father
lies next to you losing his accent

COMMUNITY

GREEN CHILE

I prefer red chile over my eggs
and potatoes for breakfast.
Red chile *ristras* decorate my door,
dry on my roof, and hang from eaves.
They lend open-air vegetable stands
historical grandeur, and gently swing
with an air of festive welcome.
I can hear them talking in the wind,
haggard, yellowing, crisp, rasping
tongues of old men, licking the breeze.

But grandmother loves green chile.
When I visit her,
she holds the green chile pepper
in her wrinkled hands.
Ah, voluptuous, masculine,
an air of authority and youth simmers
from its swan-neck stem, tapering to a flowery
collar, fermenting resinous spice.
A well-dressed gentleman at the door
my grandmother takes sensuously in her hand,
rubbing its firm glossed sides,
caressing the oily rubbery serpent,
with mouth-watering fulfillment,
fondling its curves with gentle fingers.

Its bearing magnificent and taut
as flanks of a tiger in mid-leap,
she thrusts her blade into
and cuts it open, with lust
on her hot mouth, sweating over the stove,
bandanna round her forehead,
mysterious passion on her face
and she serves me green chile con carne
between soft warm leaves of corn tortillas,
with beans and rice – her sacrifice
to her little prince.
I slurp from my plate
with last bit of tortilla, my mouth burns
and I hiss and drink a tall glass of cold water.

All over New Mexico, sunburned men and women
drive rickety trucks stuffed with gunny-sacks
of green chile, from Belen, Veguita, Willard, Estancia,
San Antonio y Socorro, from fields
to roadside stands, you see them roasting green chile
in screen-sided homemade barrels, and for a dollar
    a bag,
we relive this old, beautiful ritual again and again.

THE RUSSIAN

"The Russians had few doctors on the front line.
My father's job was this: After the battle
Was over, he'd walk among the men hit,
Sit down and ask: 'Would you like to die on your
Own in a few hours, or should I finish it?'
Most said, 'Don't leave me.' The two would have
A cigarette. He'd take out his small notebook –
We had no dog tags, you know – and write the man's
Name down, his wife's, his children, his address,
    and what
He wanted to say. When the cigarette was done,
The soldier would turn his head to the side. My father
Finished off four hundred men that way during
    the war.
He never went crazy. They were his people.

"He came to Toronto. My father in the summers
Would stand on the lawn with a hose, watering
The grass that way. It took a long time. He'd talk
To the moon, to the wind. 'I can hear you growing' –
He'd say to the grass. 'We come and go.
We're no different from each other. We are all
Part of something. We have a home.' When I was
    thirteen,
I said, 'Dad, do you know they've invented sprinklers

Now?' He went on watering the grass.
'This is my life. Just shut up if you don't understand
it.'"

A WAY OF SEEING

It all comes from this dark dirt,
memory as casual as a laborer.

Remembrances of ancestors
kept in trinkets, tiny remains

that would madden anthropologists
with their namelessness.

No records, just smells of stories
passing through most tenuous links,

trusting in the birthing of seed from seed;
this calabash bowl of Great-grand

Martha, born a slave's child;
this bundle of socks, unused

thick woolen things for the snow –
he died, Uncle Felix, before the ship

pushed off the Kingston wharf,
nosing for winter, for London.

He never used the socks, just
had them buried with him.

So, sometimes forgetting the panorama
these poems focus like a tunnel,

to a way of seeing time past,
a way of seeing the dead.

TURNING POINT

My host is a monk
from my grandfather's town,

exploring England
in a darkened age.

Stopped temporarily
in a shared room

we meet on my less
noble travels:

discover we are
exactly the same age.

At ten I knew
the world must change;

he, at ten,
also knew the same.

Twenty yards
of saffron robes

captured his boy's
imagination,

while mine slipped
on the slopes

of Tagaytay. He grew
decisive,

unencumbered
in a shaved head;

I became
progressively

less certain,
more curled.

Reaching our mid-thirties
– the age of enlightenment –

he speaks, I listen
only half understanding

this language from my past.
I have stumbled

off the path, tripped
by his inflections.

Once we had
in our Colombo house

a daylight alms-giving
feeding twenty monks.

We served, they ate.
This bright morning

at our breakfast
my laughing monk

serves me
his home-cooking,

turning the tables
in a Manchester flat.

THE OLD SCANDINAVIANS

You should hear the old Scandinavians
Singing in their white clapboard churches –
The Danes and buttoned-down Norwegians,
The tall, big-boned Swedes with shocks
Of white hair. You should hear them
Hoisting their voices from this world
To the next. I mean those bachelor farmers
Sitting in the back pews, the ones
Bellowing away in their starched collars
And same gray suits every Sunday,
Those old Carusos from Bergen, Trondheim,
The last ones left from the big crossing.
You should hear them rejoicing in their little
Drafty churches with the one-story steeples,
Under the bells that haven't rung in years.

HALF-MEXICAN

Odd to be a half-Mexican, let me put it this way
I am Mexican + Mexican, then there's the question of
the half
To say Mexican without the half, well it means
another thing
One could say only Mexican
Then think of pyramids – obsidian flaw, flame
etchings, goddesses with
Flayed visages claw feet & skulls as belts – these are
not Mexican
They are existences, that is to say
Slavery, sinew, hearts shredded sacrifices for the
continuum
Quarks & galaxies, the cosmic milk that flows into trees
Then darkness
What is the other – yes
It is Mexican too, yet it is formless, it is speckled with
particles
European pieces? To say colony or power is incorrect
Better to think of Kant in his tiny room
Shuffling in his black socks seeking out the notion
of time
Or Einstein re-working the erroneous equation
Concerning the way light bends – all this has to do with
The half, the half-thing when you are a half-being

Time

Light

How they stalk you & how you beseech them
All this becomes your life-long project, that is
You are Mexican. One half Mexican the other half
Mexican, then the half against itself.

US

If you ask me, *us* takes in *undulations* –
each wave in the sea, all insides compressed –
as if, from one coast, you could reach out to

the next; and maybe it's a Midlands thing
but when I was young, *us* equally meant *me*,
says the one, "Oi, you, tell us where yer from";

and the way supporters share the one fate –
I, being one, am *Liverpool* no less –
cresting the Mexican wave of *we* or *us*,

a shore-like state, two places at once, God
knows what's in it; and, at opposite ends
my heart's sunk at separations of *us*.

When it comes to us, colour me unsure.
Something in me, or it, has failed the course.
I'd love to think I could stretch to it – us –

but the waves therein are too wide for words.
I hope you get, here, where I'm coming from.
I hope you're with me on this – between love

and loss – where I'd give myself away, stranded
as if the universe is a matter of one stress.
Us. I hope, from here on, I can say it

and though far-fetched, it won't be too far wrong.

IN THE GLORIOUS YEMEN RESTAURANT

on Atlantic Avenue, faces kneaded
from Hadramout clay, and walls
the color of canned peaches. The men
and their moustaches come from a country
where all questions were answered
when Solomon glimpsed Sheba's thighs.
Here a man tells his story by the way
he drinks his tea. One named Anwar
asks about a charm he'd lost. His mother
tucked it in his pocket the day he left.
Mine I lost when an officer rummaged
through my clothes. My knees caved in,
my charm dubbed immigrant trash.
Haji Ahmad sits next to me because
my face is familiar. He opens an envelope,
shows me a picture of a niece's wedding.
When did you come here Haji?
He stares, puts on a reminiscent Sinbad:
I was young, took the first ship to Java.
Never returned. In Oran
a woman promised never to forget me.
In Jirba, I kissed the hand of a Jew
because his wife came from Sana'a.
I live here now, but I'm settled everywhere.
The cook wails *Ya lail, Ya lail*, a song

about tonight, how I'll walk to my room
in George and Donna's house where
Donna will be fucking another man.
Ya lail, Ya lail, Ya lail.
The waiter hands Anwar a basket
filled with lost charms – prayer beads,
photographs, false jewels. He searches
and I'm caught between laughing and weeping
because tonight I sipped sweet mint tea,
ate with my hands and licked my fingers
to satisfy a memory, to water its roots
with frankincense and cloves.
Ya lail, Ya lail. I am here, I am there,
I am lost between Carroll Street and Smith.
I slip to full moon summers,
stars dancing to the pilgrims' return.
I slip to dreams that happened in dreams.

Ya lail, which means O night!, is a common refrain in Arabic music.

THE HARLEM DANCER

Applauding youths laughed with young prostitutes
And watched her perfect, half-clothed body sway;
Her voice was like the sound of blended flutes
Blown by black players upon a picnic day.
She sang and danced on gracefully and calm,
The light gauze hanging loose about her form;
To me she seemed a proudly-swaying palm
Grown lovelier for passing through a storm.
Upon her swarthy neck black shiny curls
Luxuriant fell; and tossing coins in praise,
The wine-flushed, bold-eyed boys, and even the girls,
Devoured her shape with eager, passionate gaze;
But looking at her falsely-smiling face,
I knew her self was not in that strange place.

CLAUDE McKAY (1889 – 1948)

MAPS

For Marcelo

Some maps have blue borders
like the blue of your name
or the tributary lacing of
veins running through your
father's hands. & how the last
time I saw you, you held
me for so long I saw whole
lifetimes flooding by me
small tentacles reaching
for both our faces. I wish
maps would be without
borders & that we belonged
to no one & to everyone
at once, what a world that
would be. Or not a world
maybe we would call it
something more intrinsic
like forgiving or something
simplistic like river or dirt.
& if I were to see you
tomorrow & everyone you
came from had disappeared
I would weep with you & drown
out any black lines that this

earth allowed us to give it –
because what is a map but
a useless prison? We are all
so lost & no naming of blank
spaces can save us. & what
is a map but the delusion of
safety? The line drawn is always
in the sand & folds on itself
before we're done making it.
& that line, there, south of
el rio, how it dares to cover
up the bodies, as though we
would forget who died there
& for what? As if we could
forget that if you spin a globe
& stop it with your finger
you'll land it on top of someone
living, someone who was not
expecting to be crushed by thirst –

WHEN FIRST STARS APPEAR

My sister ties her apron, tests
the boiled cabbage with her fork,
waits for each large leaf to pull away.

Mother sits at the dinner table
guarding the candle lit for the dead.
This is not her country.
Every Epiphany she reminds us
how she lost everything.

The Bandurist Choir struggles to be heard –
the stereo needle dragging its wad of dust . . .
This year, who will praise their voices,
their dead gifts?

She tells us the same fable
of how at midnight barn animals speak . . .
My embroidered shirt irritates my neck.

Did you feed them?
Give them water?
Did you cause them pain?

I listen each time knowing
it is never the animals
that complain.

BORDER LINES

A weight carried by two
Weighs only half as much.

The world on a map looks like the drawing of a cow
In a butcher's shop, all those lines showing
Where to cut.

That drawing of the cow is also a jigsaw puzzle.
Showing just as much how very well
All the strange parts fit together.

Which way we look at the drawing
Makes all the difference.

We seem to live in a world of maps:
But in truth we live in a world made
Not of paper and ink but of people.
Those lines are our lives. Together.

Let us turn the map until we see clearly:
The border is what joins us,
Not what separates us.

ALBERTO RÍOS (1952–)

NAZIS

Thank God they're all gone
except for one or two in Clinton Maine
who come home from work
at Scott Paper or Diamond Match
to make a few crank calls
to the only Jew in New England
they can find

These make-shift students of history
whose catalogue of facts include
every Jew who gave a dollar
to elect the current governor
every Jew who'd sell this country out
to the insatiable Israeli state

I know exactly how they feel
when they say they want to smash my face

Someone's cheated them
they want to know who it is
they want to know who makes them beg
It's true Let's Be Fair
it's tough for almost everyone
I exaggerate the facts
to make a point

Just when I thought I could walk to the market
just when Jean the check-out girl
asks me how many cords of wood I chopped
and wishes me a Happy Easter
as if I've lived here all my life

Just when I can walk into the bank
and nod at the tellers who know my name
where I work who lived in my house in 1832
who know to the penny the amount
of my tiny Jewish bank account

Just when I'm sure we can all live together
and I can dine in their saltbox dining rooms
with the melancholy painting of Christ
on the wall their only consolation
just when I can borrow my neighbor's ladder
to repair one of the holes in my roof

I see the town now from the right perspective
the gunner in the glass bubble
of his fighter plane shadowing the tiny man
with the shopping bag and pointy nose
his overcoat two sizes too large for him
skulking from one doorway to the next
trying to make his own way home

I can see he's not one of us

IRA SADOFF (1945–)

AT DEB'S PARTY

The music isn't great, but in the candlelight
everything seems more sophisticated, mysterious,
even the conversation about bed sheets
with Giselle, who came already drunk.

Eric kisses Cedric.
The Polish girl and Paul
quarrel about politics
and drink vodka.

Viktor, a Ukrainian,
tells me while we dance
that he used to sell second-hand shirts
in the flea market in Baia Mare.

Natasha, an Australian,
consoles Giselle and tells her
she has to do something with her life
besides sobbing and vomiting.

Look around, Giselle, don't you see,
this is why we left our countries:
life was running through our fingers,
and here, it still does.

I go to the kitchen to look for some ice,
and I'm thinking this is why
you came from Australia, Natasha,
and I from Romania:

to save Giselle from drowning.

MY FATHER EATS FIGS

My father eats figs
the way he eats his past,
spits out the skin.

He eats figs and stares
out the window at Mrs. Grimm's
curtains: she knows

our secret, how we emerged
from the jungle. She watches me
with green eyes and razor lips.

Witch, djinn, she eats children
and buries their bones
in her backyard – I've been there.

My father eats figs
the way he and his father
ate eggs on the farm

of the other world:
boiled in their shells –
peeled and swallowed

whole, devouring a hundred
at a time. He eats figs, watches
my sister and me, white tulle

and ballet shoes, arms raised,
as we pirouette
on broken pavement.

Mom mans the record player.
Neighbors watch.
Dancing dolls with painted

cheeks, swaying like the palms
we've already forgotten.
The phone rings – Dad runs inside.

We dance and dance,
and it's years
before we see him again.

GREAT GRANDFATHERS FROM SZUMSK OFFER ADVICE TO MY CHILDREN

Instead of using the staircase, risk
the tendrilled stalks of ivy
and drop into the muddy copse below.

We, great grandfathers, knew mud
as we slogged from village to village
peddling pots and ribbons and scissors.

We faced days with no light, nights
with no heat, years with no safety –
years of pogroms, famine, and loss.

But, still, you may collar our essence
if, shaking pearls from your ears,
you can know wet boots and windfall.

DAUGHTER-MOTHER-MAYA-SEETA

To replay errors
the revolving door of days
Now it's over
There's no one point thank god in the turning world
I was always moving
tired too but laughing
To be a widow is an old
freedom I have known
vidua paradisea   a bird
Singly I flew
and happiness was my giraffe
in the face of Africa
me among daughters
and my son at work
me pregnant with them
taking in the glamour days
town and country mirabella elle vogue
cosmopolitan   We have made this world
brown these beautiful women
laughing and crying till we cleared the dining table
In hotels men asked my girls to fetch them towels
In restaurants they asked us for bread
Today I'm a civil servant on the Hill

From the Mall what colorful sarongs
my children bring to drape my ankles
the gifts we give
to Mina a necklace of Mikimoto pearls
Tara a Paloma purse for cosmetics
Lata a pair of lime shoes for the miles
Devi gives me her eclectic lit eyes
the glamour of our wilder regions
Bombay weavers on the twenty-four hour looms
shocking pink is the navy of India

Listen I am listening
my mind is a trip
I flew over oceans
I flew in the face of skies
orienting my loss of caste
my dark complexion
the folly of envy
wishing all my life to be fair
My jealous god leaves
Hello son this is your mother
Daughters take these maroon saris
these maroon bras
I am proud to have borne you
When you gather around me
newness comes into the world

ACKNOWLEDGMENTS

Thanks are due to the following copyright holders for permission to reprint:

JOHN AGARD: "The Embodiment" from *Alternative Anthems: Selected Poems with Live DVD* (Bloodaxe Books, 2009). Reproduced with permission from Bloodaxe Books, www.bloodaxebooks.com. DILRUBA AHMED: "Dear Masoom" from *Dhaka Dust*. Originally published in *Catamaran: South Asian American Writing*. Copyright © 2011 by Dilruba Ahmed. Reprinted with the permission of The Permissions Company, LLC on behalf of Graywolf Press, graywolfpress.org. NEIL AITKEN: "Outside Plato's Republic, The Last Poets Wait for Departure" from *The Lost Country of Sight* (Anhinga Press, 2008). Reprinted with permission from Anhinga Press and the poet. KAVEH AKBAR: "Do You Speak Persian?" from *Calling a Wolf a Wolf*. Copyright © 2017 by Kaveh Akbar. Reprinted with the permission of The Permissions Company, LLC on behalf of Alice James Books, alicejamesbooks.org. AGHA SHAHID ALI: "Of It All" from *The Veiled Suite*, W. W. Norton & Co. KAZIM ALI: "Ursa Major" from *The Fortieth Day*. Copyright © 2008 by Kazim Ali. Reprinted with the permission of The Permissions Company, LLC on behalf of BOA Editions Ltd, boaeditions.org. MONIZA ALVI: "Rural Scene" from *Split World: Poems 1990–2005* (Bloodaxe Books, 2008). Reproduced with permission of Bloodaxe Books, www.bloodaxebooks.com. INDRAN AMIRTHANAYAGAM: "The Migrant's Reply" from *The Migrant States*, Hanging Loose Press, 2020. Reprinted with permission from the author. MONA ARSHI: "The Daughters" from *Small Hands*, Liverpool University Press, 2015. RUTH AWAD: "Town Gossip" from *Set to Music a Wildfire*, published by the University of Southern Indiana. Reprinted with permission from Southern Indiana Review and the poet. JIMMY SANTIAGO BACA: "Green Chile" from *Black Mesa Poems*, New Directions Publishing Corp. SHAUNA BARBOSA: "Broke" from *Cape Verdean Blues* by Shauna Barbosa, © 2018. Reprinted by permission of the University of Pittsburgh Press. HADARA BAR-NADAV: "Chest" from *The New Nudity*, Saturnalia Books. Copyright © 2017 Hadara Bar-Nadav. LORY BEDIKIAN: "The Mechanic" from *The Book of Lamenting*, Anhinga Press, 2011. Copyright © 2011 by Lory Bedikian. JAMES BERRY: "Roomseeker in London" from *Fractured Circles*, New Beacon Press, 1979. ROBERT BLY: "The Russian" from *Eating the Honey of Words*, HarperFlamingo, a division of HarperCollins, Publishers. LAURE-ANNE BOSSELAAR: "English Flavors" from *The Hour Between Dog and Wolf*. Copyright © 1997 by Laure-Anne Bosselaar. Reprinted with the permission of The Permissions Company, LLC on behalf of BOA Editions, Ltd, boaeditions.org. KAMAU BRATHWAITE: Section 11 from "Guanahani" from *Born to Slow Horses*, Wesleyan University Press, 2005. MICHAEL BROEK: "The Golden Venture" from *Refuge/es*. Copyright © 2015 by Michael Broek. Reprinted with the permission of The Permissions Company, LLC on behalf of Alice James Books, alicejamesbooks.org. CHRISTIAN CAMPBELL: "Iguana" from *Running the Dusk*, Peepal Tree Press, 2010. RAFAEL CAMPO: "My Voice" from *What the Body Told*, Duke University Press, 1996. MARCELO HERNANDEZ CASTILLO: "Immigration Interview with Don Francisco" from *Cenzontle*. Copyright © 2018 by Marcelo Hernandez Castillo. Reprinted with the permission of The Permissions Company, LLC on behalf of BOA Editions Ltd, boaeditions.org. MARY JEAN CHAN: "Rules for a Chinese Child Buying Stationery in a London Bookshop" from *Flèche*. Faber & Faber Limited.

ANDRÉE CHEDID: "My Rediscovered Land" translated by Kathryn Kimball, from *L'Etoffe de l'univers,* © Flammarion. Translation copyright © by Kathryn Kimball. Reprinted with permission. ANDREI CODRESCU: "ah, ach, vai bilingvism" from *The Art of Forgetting,* Sheep Meadow Press. EDUARDO C. CORRAL: "Immigration and Naturalization Service Report #46" from *Slow Lightning,* Yale University Press. FRED D'AGUIAR: "Home" from *British Subjects,* Bloodaxe Books. Copyright © Fred D'Aguiar. MAHMOUD DARWISH: "The Passport" from *Splinters of Bone.* The Greenfield Review Press, 1974. KWAME DAWES: "A Way of Seeing" from *Jacko Jacobus,* Peepal Tree Press, 1996. IMTIAZ DHARKER: "How to cut a pomegranate" from *The Terrorist at My Table* (Bloodaxe Books, 2006). Reproduced with permission of Bloodaxe Books, www.bloodaxebooks.com. GREGORY DJANIKIAN: "When I First Saw Snow" from *Falling Deeply Into America,* Carnegie Mellon University Press, 1989. Reprinted with permission. INUA ELLAMS: "GuerillaGardenWritingPoem" from *Untitled* (Oberon Books, 2005). Copyright © by Inua Ellams. Reprinted with permission from the poet. KATHY ENGEL: "What could the title possibly be". Copyright © by Kathy Engel. Reprinted with permission from the poet. ALEJANDRO ESCOVEDO: "Wave". Copyright © BMG Rights Management. RHINA P. ESPAILLAT: "Bilingual/Bilingue" from *Where Horizons Go* (New Odyssey Press, 1998). Reprinted with permission from Truman State University Press. BERNADINE EVARISTO: Excerpt "Taiwo" [45 lines] from *Lara* (Bloodaxe Books, 2009). Reproduced with permission of Bloodaxe Books, www.bloodaxebooks.com. TARFIA FAIZULLAH: "To the Bangladeshi Cab Driver in San Francisco" from *Registers of Illuminated Villages.* Copyright © 2018 by Tarfia Faizullah. Reprinted with the permission of The Permissions Company, LLC on behalf of Graywolf Press, graywolfpress.org. JAWDAT FAKHREDDINE: "Land" from *Lighthouse For The Drowning*, translated by Jayson Iwen and Huda Fakhreddine. Copyright © 1996 by Jawdat Fakhreddine. English translation copyright © 2017 by Jayson Iwen and Huda Fakhreddine. Reprinted with the permission of The Permissions Company, LLC on behalf of BOA Editions, Ltd, boaeditions.org. CARMEN FIRAN: "How I Am" from *Born in Utopia*, Talisman House Publishers. MARISA FRASCA: "Anise Seed" from *Wild Fennel: Poems & Other Stories*, Bordighera Press, 2019. ARACELIS GIRMAY: "The Fig Eaters, Fifth Estrangement" from *The Black Maria*. Copyright © 2016 by Aracelis Girmay. Reprinted with the permission of The Permissions Company, LLC on behalf of BOA Editions Ltd, boaeditions.org. ALBERT GOLDBARTH: "*Shoyn Fergéssin*: 'I've Forgotten' in Yiddish" reprinted with permission of the poet. RAY GONZALEZ: "Was Federico García Lorca Lonely in New York?" from *The Heat of Arrivals*. Copyright © 1996 by Ray Gonzalez. Reprinted with the permission of The Permissions Company, LLC on behalf of BOA Editions Ltd, boaeditions.org. LORNA GOODISON: "Making Life" from *Controlling the Silver*, University of Illinois Press. RICHARD GRANT: "Fires burn in Bradford, Rockstone fling innah Oldham" from *Out of Bounds* (Bloodaxe Books). Dreadlockalien, Birmingham Poet Laureate 2005. Reprinted with permission from the poet. ROMESH GUNESEKERA: "Turning Point" from *The Redbeck Anthology of British South Asian Poetry* (Redbeck Press, 2000). KIMIKO HAHN: "A Flushing Villanelle". Copyright © by Kimiko Hahn. Reprinted with permission. MAGGIE HARRIS: 'Llamas, Cwmpengraig' from *After A Visit to A Botanical Garden* (Cane Arrow Press, 2010). Reprinted with permission from Cane Arrow Press. LORRAINE HEALY: "The country I flee from daily" from *The Habit of*

Buenos Aires by Lorraine Healy, Tebot Bach, 2010. ROBERT HEDIN: "The Old Scandinavians" from *At the Great Door of Morning: Selected Poems and Translations.* Copyright © 2017 by Robert Hedin. Reprinted with the permission of The Permissions Company, LLC on behalf of Copper Canyon Press, coppercanyonpress.org. JUAN FELIPE HERRERA: "Half-Mexican" from *Notes on the Assemblage.* Copyright © 2015 by Juan Felipe Herrera. Reprinted with the permission of The Permissions Company, LLC on behalf of City Lights Books, www.citylights.com. WILLIAM HEYEN: "A Snapshot of My Father, 1928" from *The Candle: Holocaust Poems 1970–2015.* Copyright © 1977, 2016 by William Heyen. Reprinted with the permission of The Permissions Company, LLC, on behalf of Etruscan Press, etruscanpress.org. HA JIN: "Bargain" from *Facing Shadows,* Hanging Loose Press, 1996. ALLISON JOSEPH: "Immigrants" from *Soul Train,* Carnegie Mellon University Press, 1997. Copyright © by Allison Joseph. JANINE JOSEPH: "Assimilation" from *Driving Without a License.* Copyright © 2016 by Janine Joseph. Reprinted with the permission of The Permissions Company, LLC on behalf of Alice James Books, alicejamesbooks.org. HÉDY KADDOUR: "The Night Watchman" translated by Marilyn Hacker, from *Treason: Poems by Hédi Kaddour.* Yale University Press. ILYA KAMINSKY: "Elegy for Joseph Brodsky" from *Dancing in Odessa.* Copyright © 2004 by Ilya Kaminsky. Reprinted with the permission of The Permissions Company, LLC on behalf of Tupelo Press, tupelopress.org. ROLANDO KATTAN: "The Pineapple Tree" translated by Nicolette Reim. Copyright © 2018 by Rolando Kattan. Reprinted with permission from the poet. Translation copyright © 2018 by Nicolette Reim. Reprinted with permission from the translator. JACKIE KAY: "In my country" from *Darling: New & Selected Poems* (Bloodaxe Books, 2007).

Reproduced with permission of Bloodaxe Books, www.bloodaxebooks.com. ANNIE KIM: "Map of Korea, 1950" from *Into the Cyclorama*, published by the University of Southern Indiana. Reprinted with permission from Southern Indiana Review and the poet. CHRISTINE KITANO: "For the Korean Grandmother on Sunset Boulevard" from *Sky Country*. Copyright © 2017 by Christine Kitano. Reprinted with the permission of The Permissions Company, LLC on behalf of BOA Editions Ltd, boaeditions.org. ZAFFAR KUNIAL: "Us" from *Us* (Faber & Faber). Rogers, Coleridge & White. TATO LAVIERA: "AmeRícan" from *AmeRícan*, Arte Publico Press. LI-YOUNG LEE: "Persimmons" from *Rose*. Copyright © 1986 by Li-Young Lee. Reprinted with the permission of The Permissions Company, LLC on behalf of BOA Editions Ltd, boaeditions.org. PHILIP LEVINE: "On the Birth of Good & Evil During the Long Winter of '28" from *New Selected Poems* by Philip Levine, copyright © 1984, 1991 by Philip Levine. Used by permission of Alfred A. Knopf, an imprint of the Knopf Doubleday Publishing Group, a division of Penguin Random House LLC. All rights reserved. SHIRLEY GEOK-LIN LIM: "Starlight Haven" from *What The Fortune Teller Didn't Say* by Shirley Geok-lin Lim, West End Press. Copyright © 1998 by Shirley Geok-lin Lim. Reprinted with permission from the author. ADA LIMÓN: "The Contract Says: We'd Like the Conversation to Be Bilingual" from *The Carrying*, Milkweed Editions, 2018. ESTHER LIN: "Illegal Immigration". Reprinted with permission of the author. NICK MAKOHA: "Stone". Reprinted with permission from the poet. JACK MAPANJE: "After Celebrating Our Asylum Stories at West Yorkshire Playhouse, Leeds" from *Last of the Sweet Bananas: New & Selected Poems* (Bloodaxe Books, 2004). Reproduced with permission of Bloodaxe Books, www.bloodaxebooks.com.

J. MICHAEL MARTINEZ: "Lord, Spanglish Me" from *Museum of the Americas* by J. Michael Martinez, copyright © 2018 by J. Michael Martinez. Used by permission of Penguin Books, an imprint of Penguin Publishing Group, a division of Penguin Random House LLC. All rights reserved. KHALED MATTAWA: "In the Glorious Yemen Restaurant" from *Ismailia Eclipse*, Sheep Meadow Press, 1995. SHARA McCALLUM: "Psalm for Kingston" from *This Strange Land.* Copyright © 2011 by Shara McCallum. Reprinted with the permission of The Permissions Company, LLC on behalf of Alice James Books, alicejamesbooks.org. CLAUDE McKAY: "The Harlem Dancer" from *Complete Poems,* University of Illinois Press. RO MEHROOZ: "Broken Mirror" from *I am a Rohingya*, Arc Publications, 2019. DUNYA MIKHAIL: Excerpt [8 lines] from *The Iraqi Nights,* New Directions Publishing Corp. KEI MILLER: "The only thing far away" from *There is an Anger That Moves,* Carcanet Press, 2007. Reprinted with permission. CZESLAW MILOSZ: "My Faithful Mother Tongue" from *New and Collected Poems, 1931–2001,* Ecco Press, a division of HarperCollins, Publishers. YESENIA MONTILLA: "Maps", copyright © by Yesenia Montilla. VALZHYNA MORT: "Belarusian I" from *Collected Body.* Copyright © 2010, 2011 by Valzhyna Mort. Reprinted with the permission of The Permissions Company, LLC on behalf of Copper Canyon Press, coppercanyonpress.org. WIDAD NABI: "The Place Is Lit with Memory", translated from Arabic by Ali Znaidi. AIMEE NEZHUKUMATATHIL: "Fishbone" from *Miracle Fruit.* Copyright © 2003 by Aimee Nezhukumatathil. Reprinted with the permission of The Permissions Company, LLC on behalf of Tupelo Press, tupelopress.org. D. NURKSE: "In the Hold" from *The Border Kingdom: Poems* by D. Nurkse, copyright © 2008 by D. Nurkse. Used by permission of Alfred A. Knopf, an imprint of the Knopf Doubleday Publishing Group, a division of Penguin Random House LLC. All rights reserved. NAOMI SHIHAB NYE: "Arabic" from *Red Suitcase.* Copyright © 1994 by Naomi Shihab Nye. Reprinted with the permission of The Permissions Company, LLC on behalf of BOA Editions Ltd, boaeditions.org. PETER ORESICK: "Ruthenia" from *Iconoscope: New and Selected Poems* by Peter Oresick, © 2015. Reprinted by permission of the University of Pittsburgh Press. DZVINIA ORLOWSKY: "When First Stars Appear" from *A Handful of Bees*, Carnegie Mellon University Press, 1994. Reprinted with permission. ALICIA SUSKIN OSTRIKER: "Guyana: So Nice" from *Waiting for the Light* by Alicia Suskin Ostriker, © 2017. Reprinted by permission of the University of Pittsburgh Press. RUTH PADEL: "The Prayer Labyrinth" from *On Migration*, Counterpoint Press, 2013. BAO PHI: "Adrift" originally published in *Poem-a-Day* (24th September 2018), by the Academy of American Poets. Copyright © 2018 by Bao Phi. Reprinted with permission from the poet. SHAMPA RAY: "My India" from *Out of Bounds* (Bloodaxe Books). Berlinn/Polygon. ALBERTO RÍOS: "Border Lines" from *A Small Story About the Sky.* Copyright © 2015 by Alberto Ríos. Reprinted with the permission of The Permissions Company, LLC on behalf of Copper Canyon Press, coppercanyonpress.org. IRA SADOFF: "Nazis" from *Emotional Traffic* by Ira Sadoff. Copyright © Ira Sadoff, 1990. Reprinted with the permission of David R. Godine, Publisher, 1990. OMAR SAKR: "Where I am Not" originally published in *Poem-a-Day* (4th September 2019), by the Academy of American Poets. Copyright © 2019 by Omar Sakr. Reprinted with permission. ADRIAN SANGEORZAN: "Underground Pearls" from *Over the Lifetime*, Spuyten Duyvil, 2003. DON SCHOFIELD: "Migrant Stories" from *The Flow of Wonder.* Kelsay Books. Copyright © by Don Schofield.

Reprinted with permission from Kelsay Books and Don Schofield. ROGER SEDERAT: "Dear Regime" from *Dear Regime: Letters to the Islamic Republic*, Ohio University Press, 2013. CLAUDIA SEREA: "At Deb's Party" from *To Part Is To Die A Little*, Cervena Barva Press, 2013. Copyright © by Claudia Serea. Reprinted with permission from Cervena Barva Press and Claudia Serea. RUTH KNAFO SETTON: "My Father Eats Figs". Copyright © by Ruth Knafo Setton. Reprinted with permission from the poet. www.ruthknafosetton.com. WARSAN SHIRE: "Midnight in the Foreign Food Aisle" from *Her Blue Body*. JACOB SHORES-ARGÜELLO: "Workshop". Copyright © by Jacob Shores-Argüello. Reprinted with permission. MARIANA SIERRA: "Mangoes at Kroger". Reprinted with permission from the poet. CHARLES SIMIC: "Explorers" from *Selected Early Poems*. Copyright © 1969 by Charles Simic. Reprinted with the permission of George Braziller, Inc. (New York), www.georgebraziller.com. All rights reserved. CARMEN GIMÉNEZ SMITH: "Southern Cone" from *Be Recorder*. Copyright © 2019 by Carmen Giménez Smith. Reprinted with the permission of The Permissions Company, LLC on behalf of Graywolf Press, graywolfpress.org. SANDY SOLOMON: "Political Refugee, One Month On" from *Pears, Lake, Sun* by Sandy Solomon. University of Pittsburgh Press. CATHY SONG: "Picture Bride" from *Picture Bride*, Yale University Press. GARY SOTO: "Mexicans Begin Jogging" from *New & Selected Poems*, Chronicle Books, 1995. GERALD STERN: "The Dancing" from *Early Collected Poems*, W. W. Norton & Co. ADRIENNE SU: "Peaches" originally published in *Poem-a-Day* (23rd October 2015), by the Academy of American Poets. Copyright © 2015 by Adrienne Su. FADWA SULEIMAN: "Laurel" (translated by Marilyn Hacker) from *Blazons: New and Selected Poems, 2000–2018*, Carcanet Press, 2019. Reprinted with permission.